Fancy Coloring

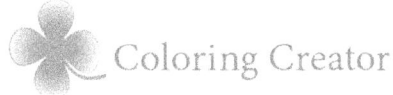

All rights reserved. No part of this publication may be reproduced, stored in retrieval system, copied in any form or by any means, electronic, mechanical, photocopying, recording or otherwise transmitted without written permission from the publisher.
Please do not participate in or encourage piracy of this material in any way. You must not circulate this book in any format.

Coloring Creater does not control or direct users' actions and is not responsible for the information or content shared, harm and/ or actions of the book readers.

ISBN-13:
978-1977863355

ISBN-10:
1977863353

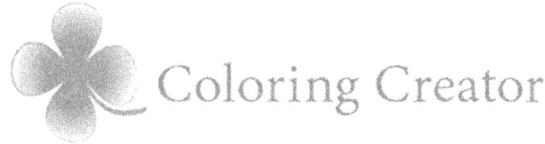

COLOR TEST PAGE

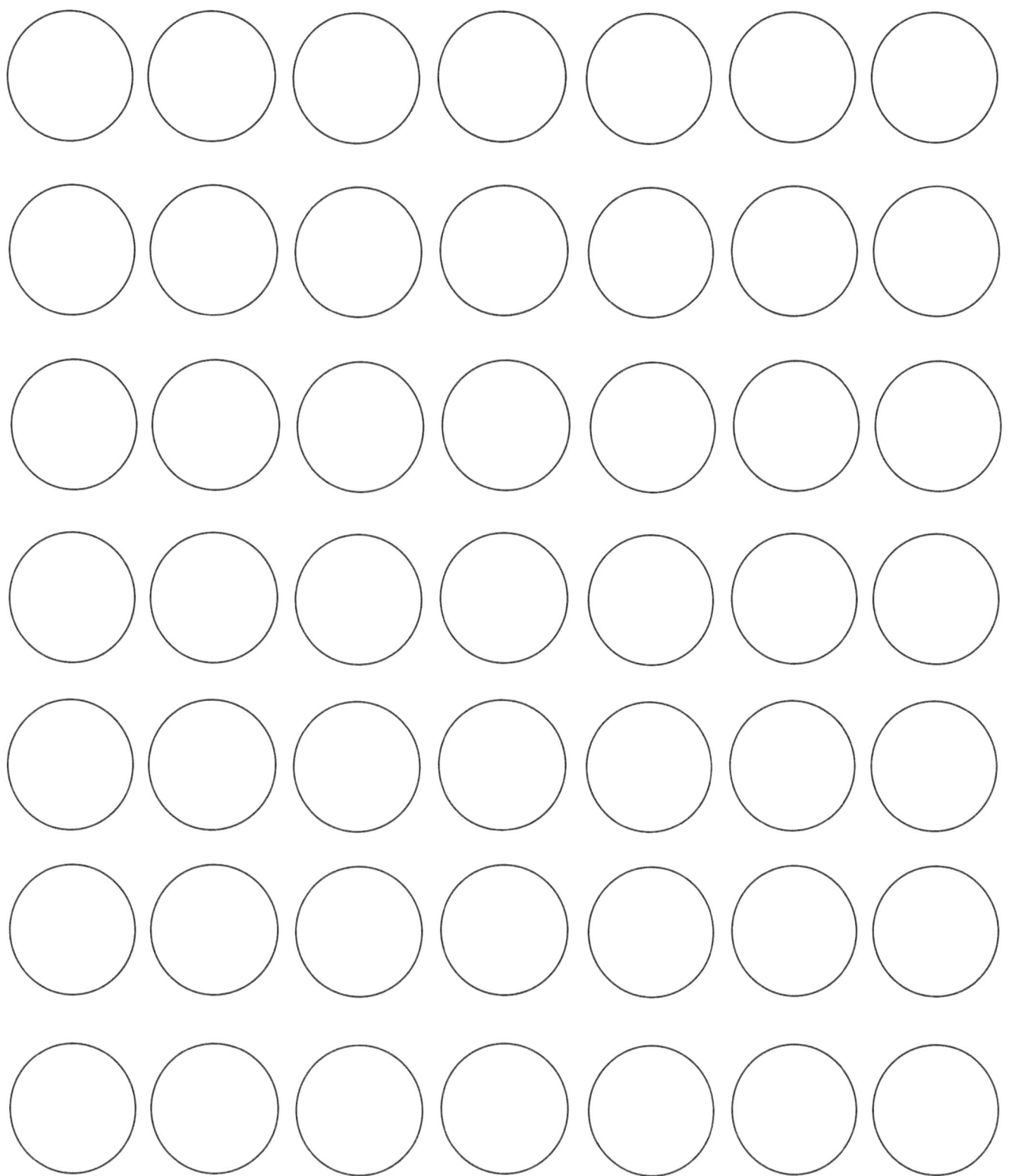

Copyrighted Material

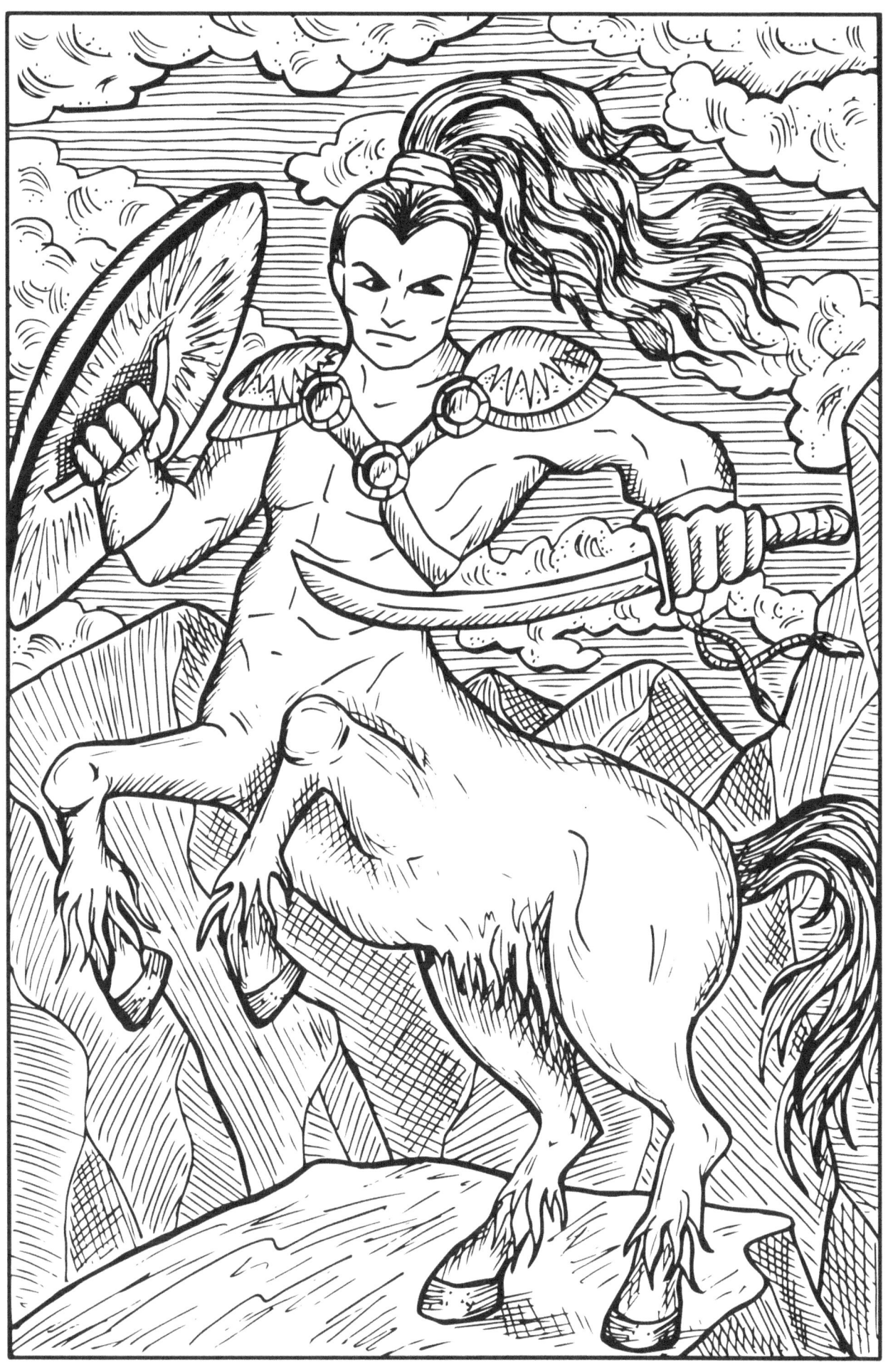

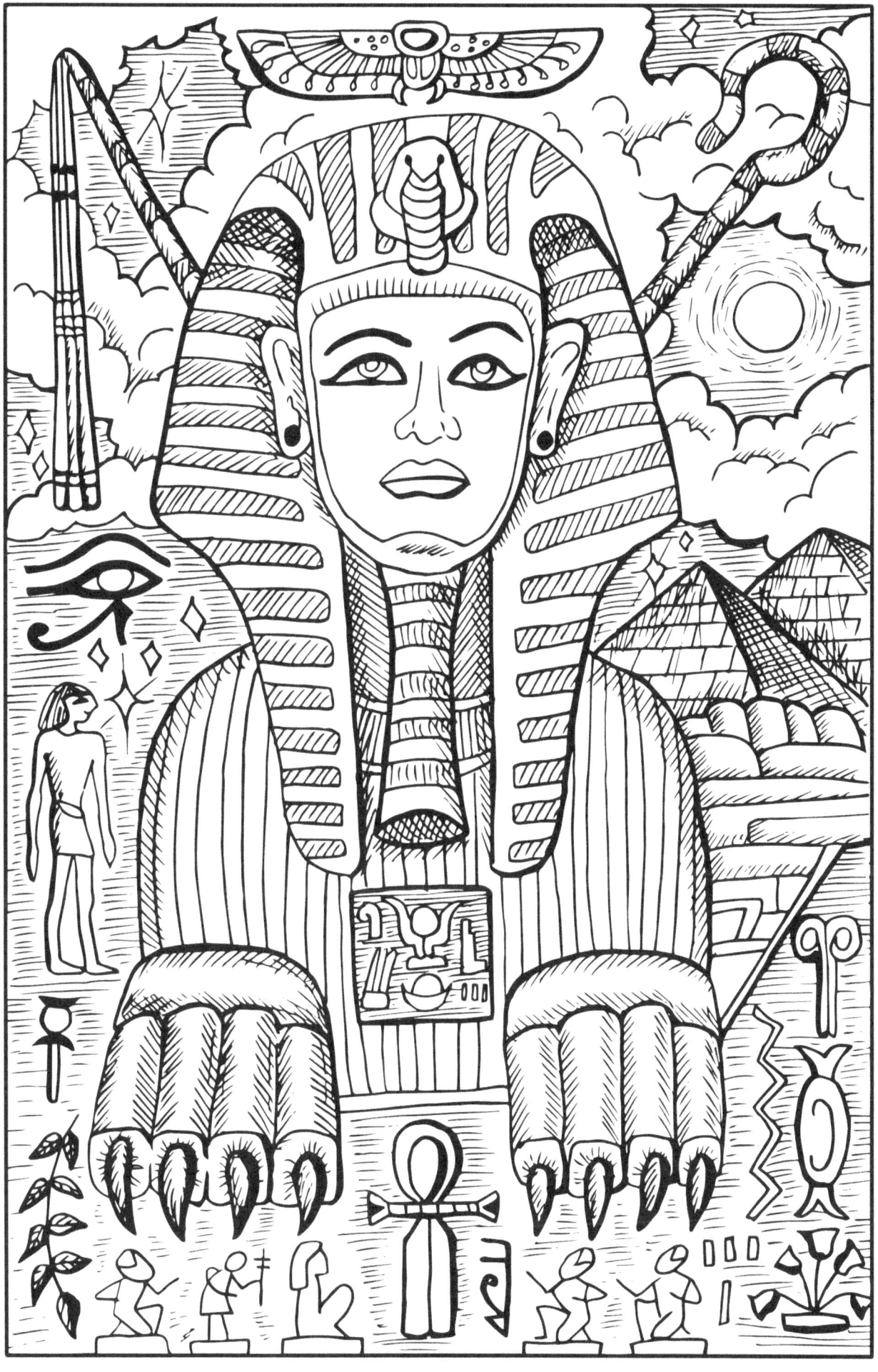

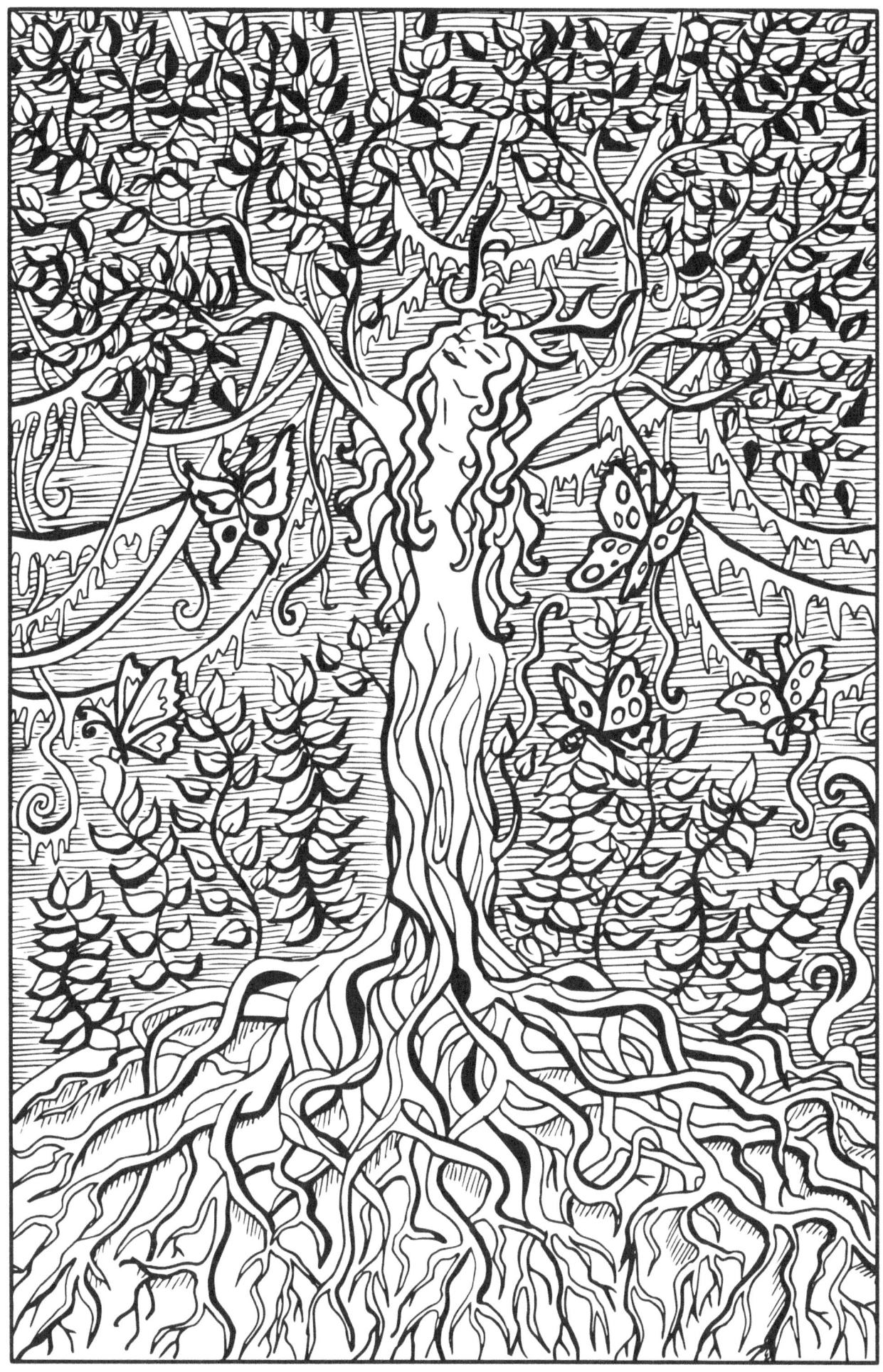

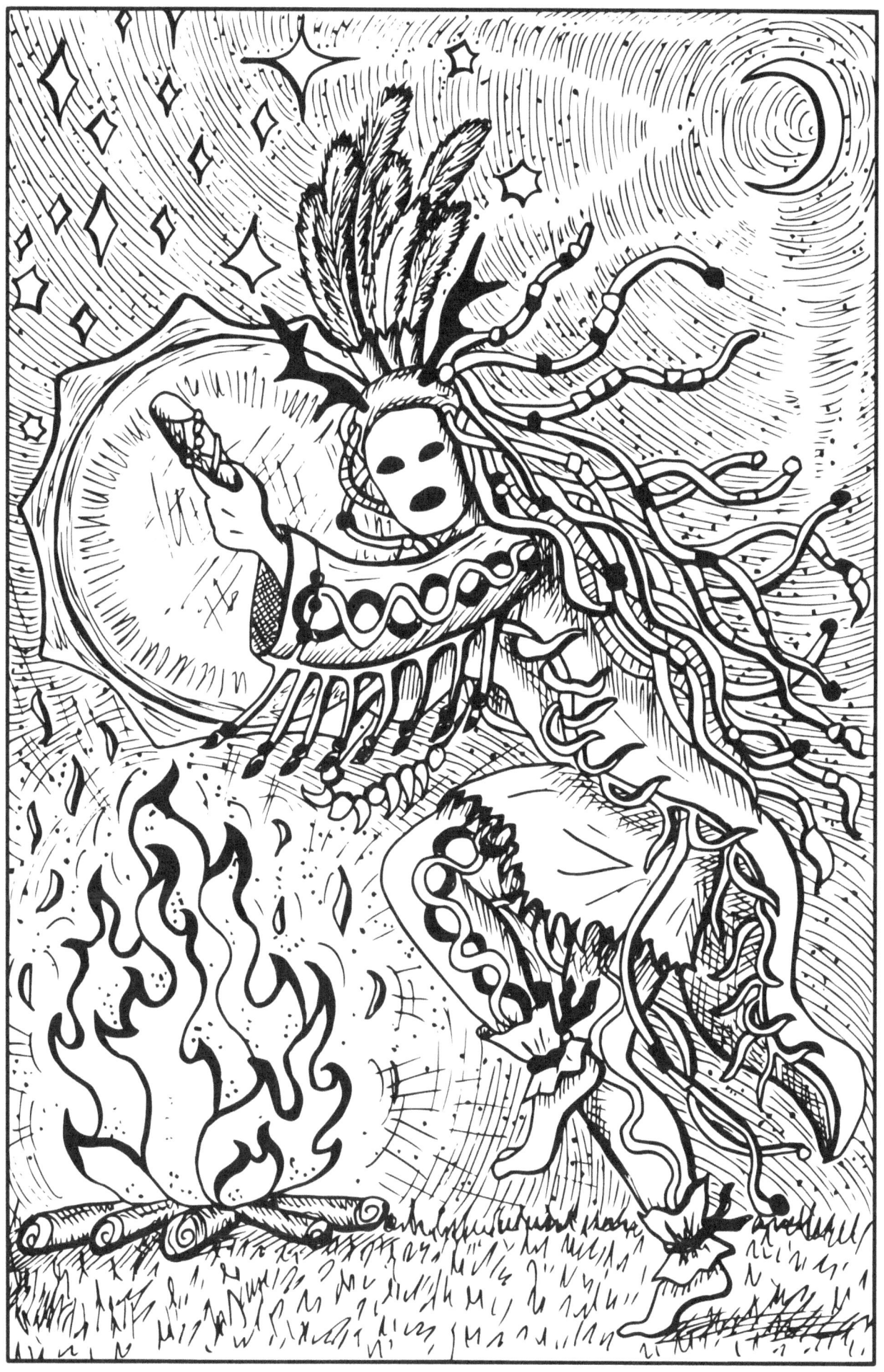

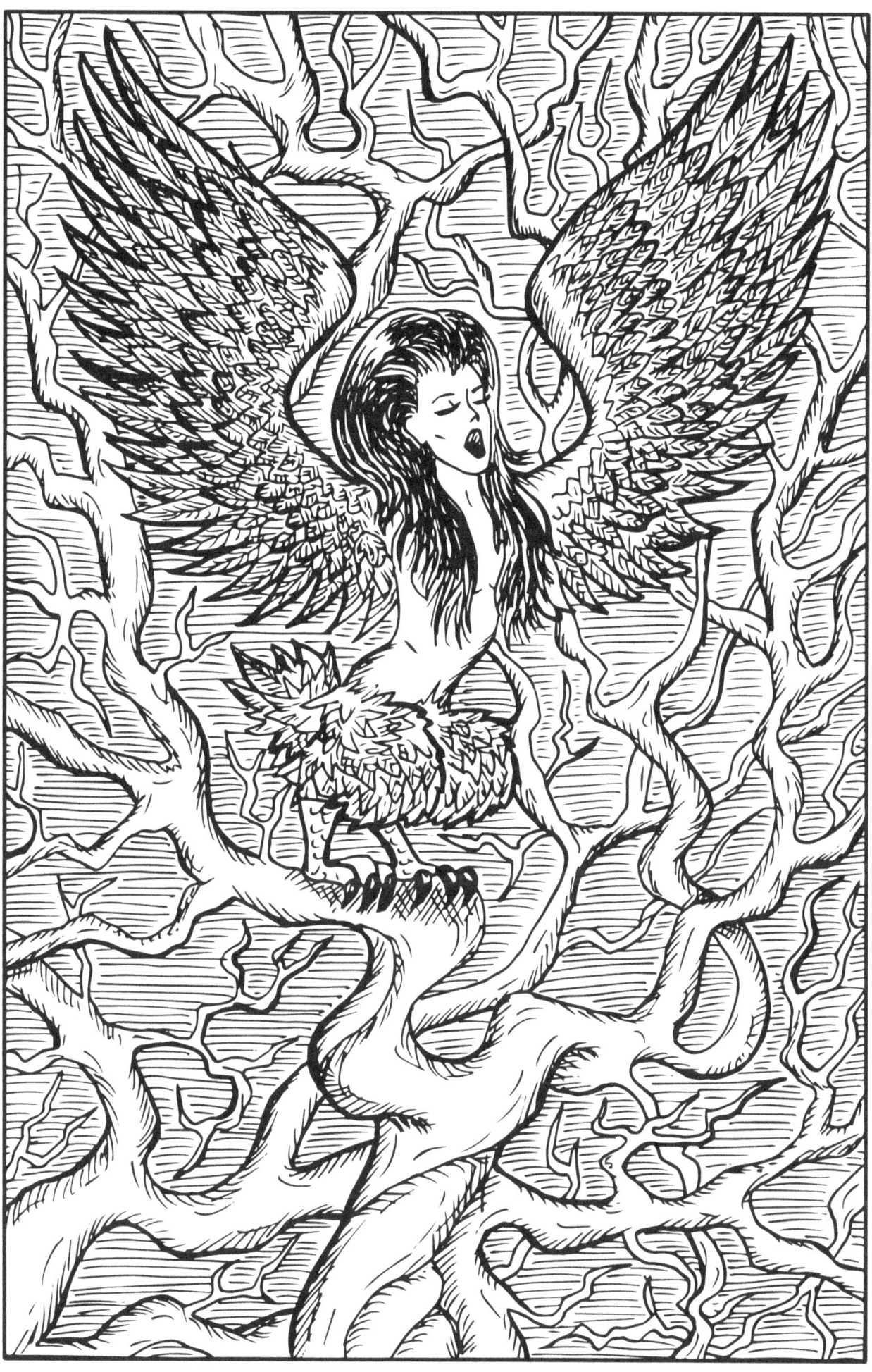

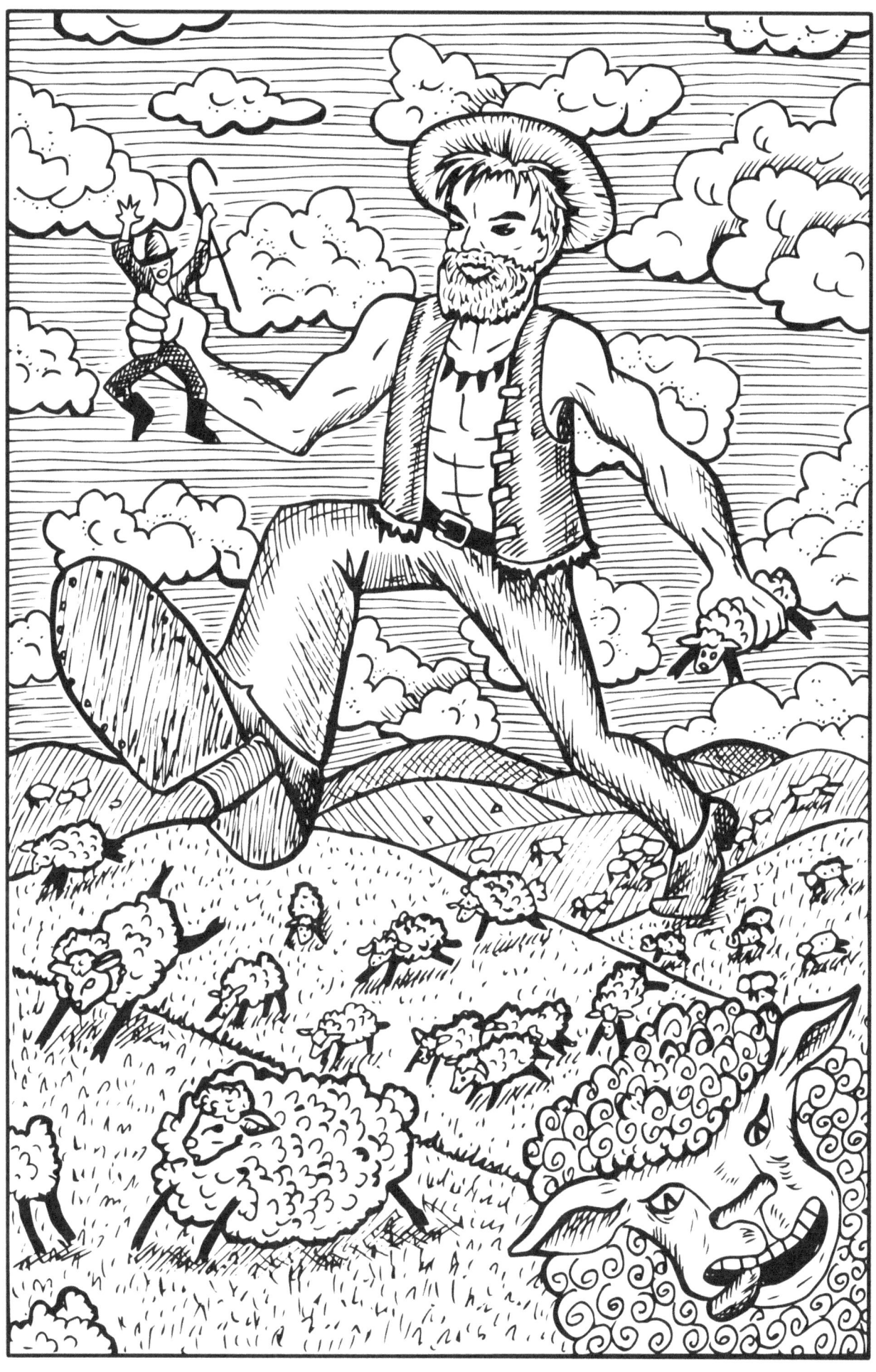

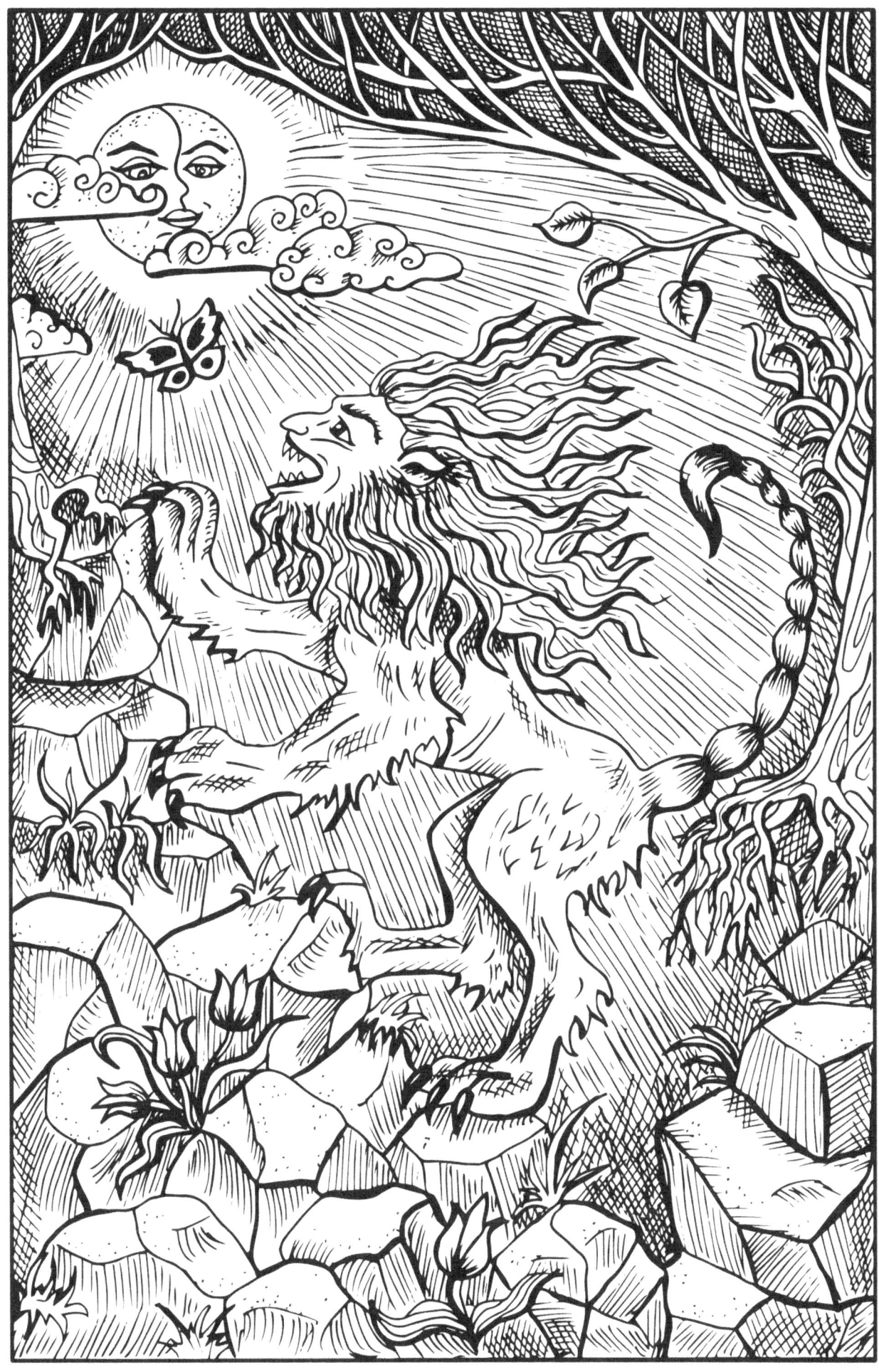

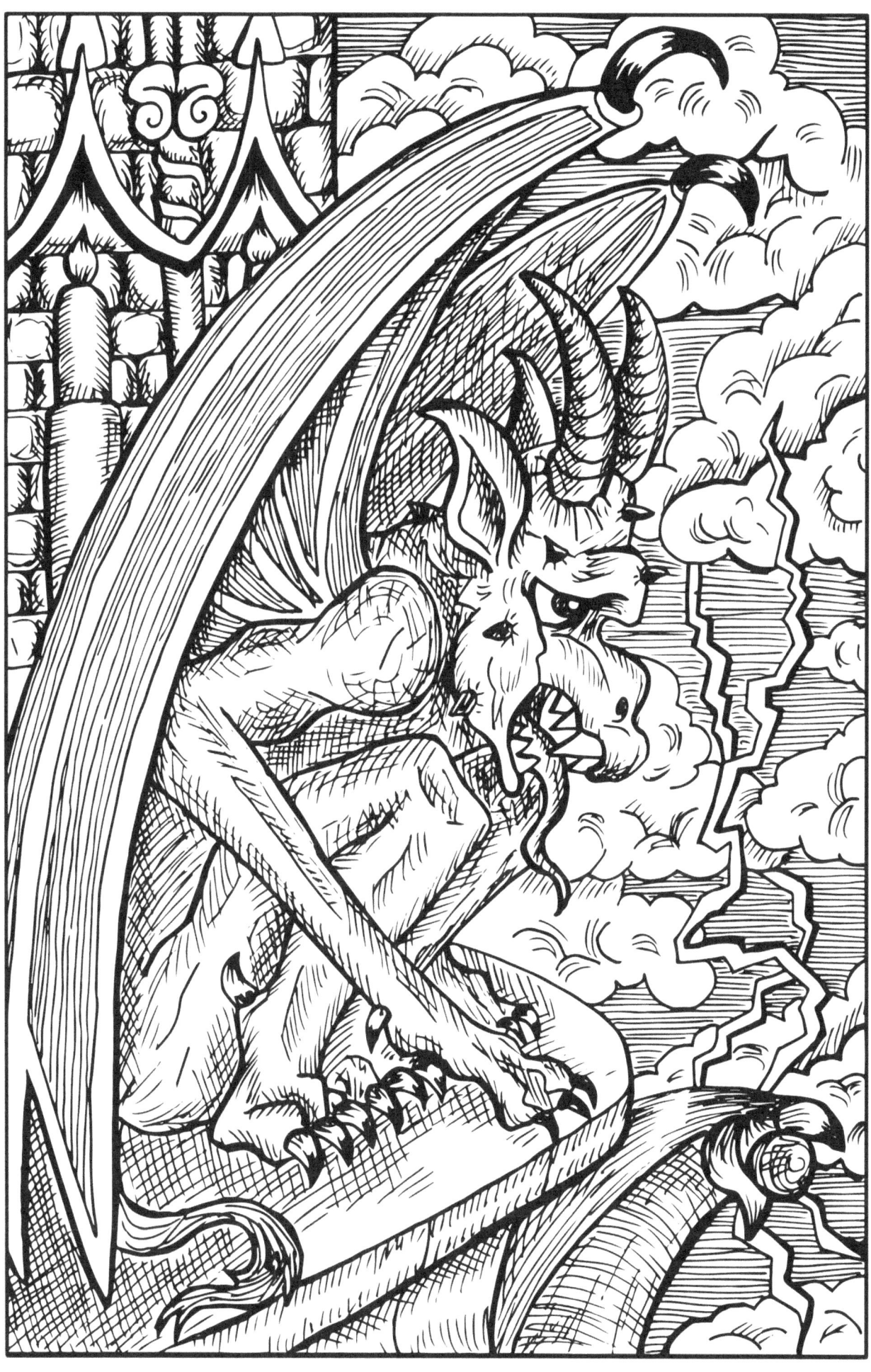

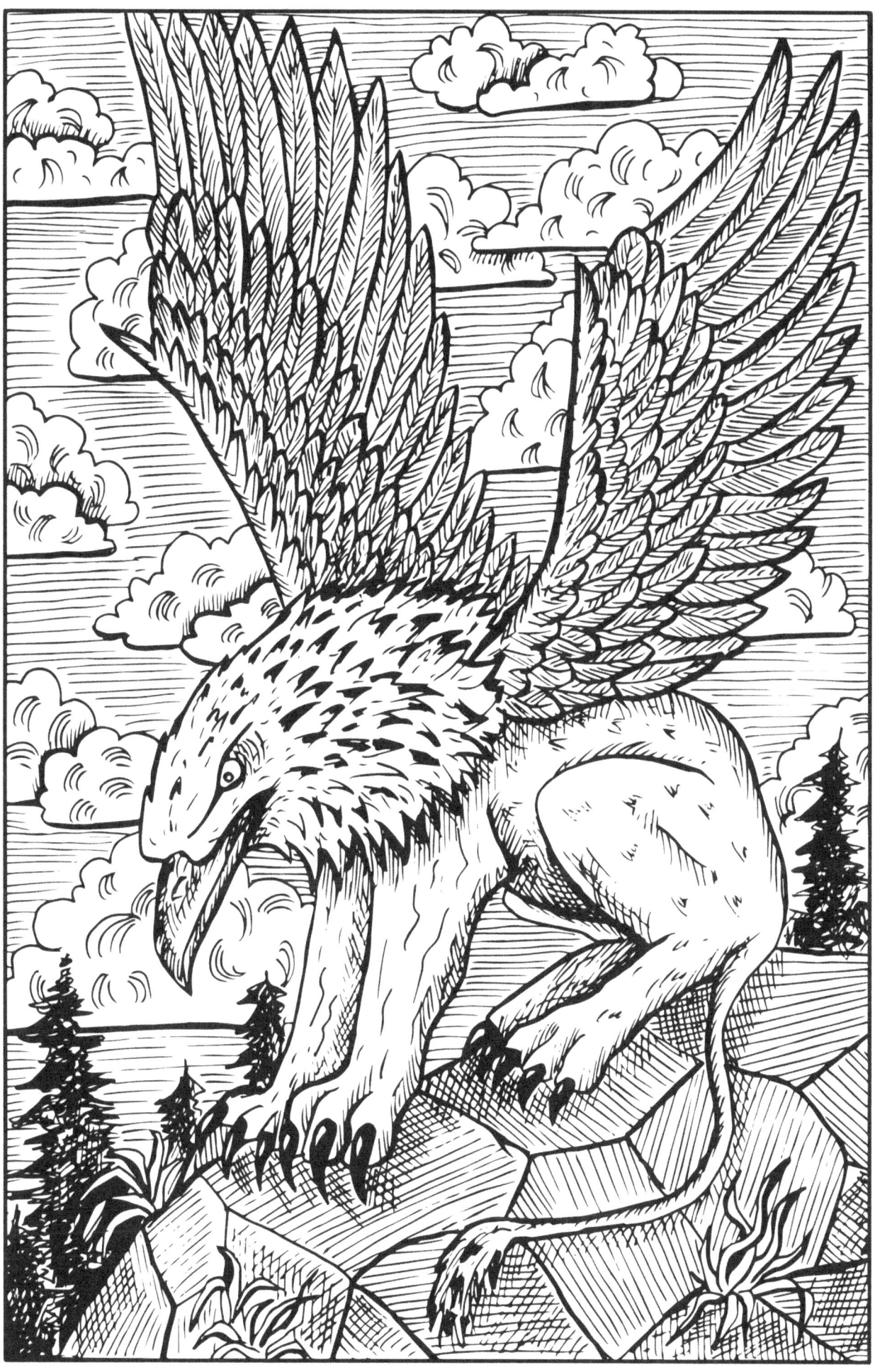

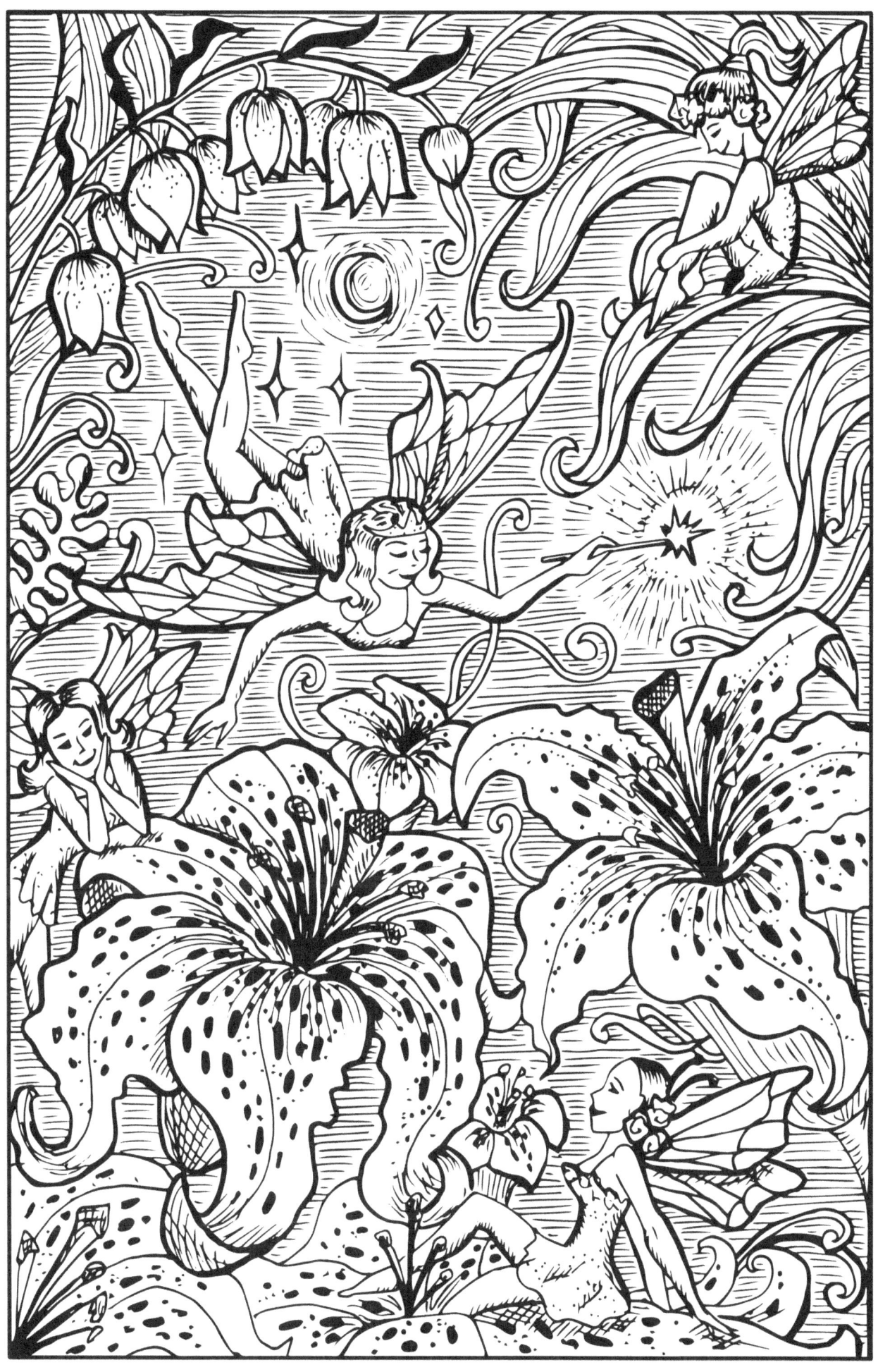

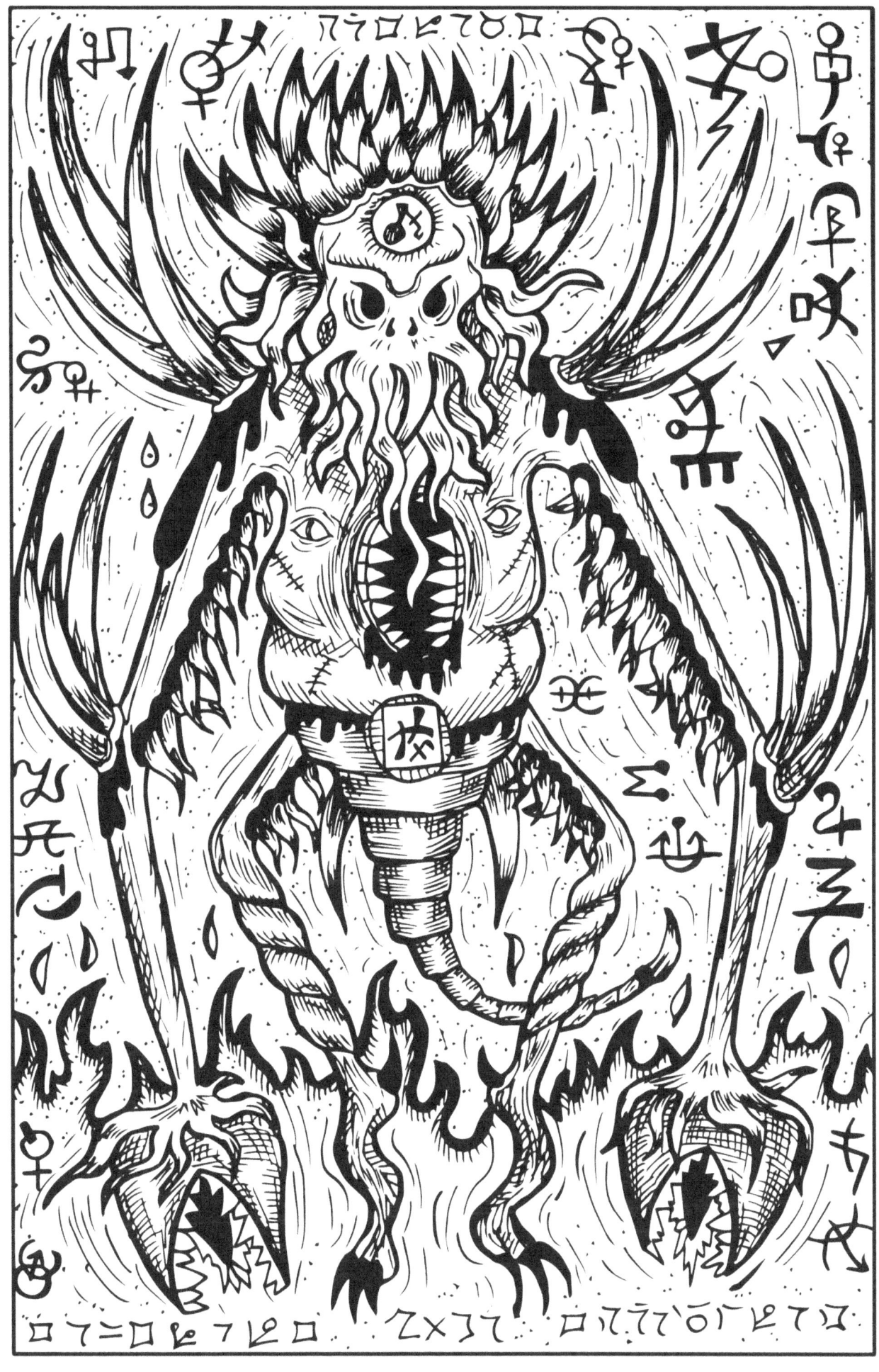

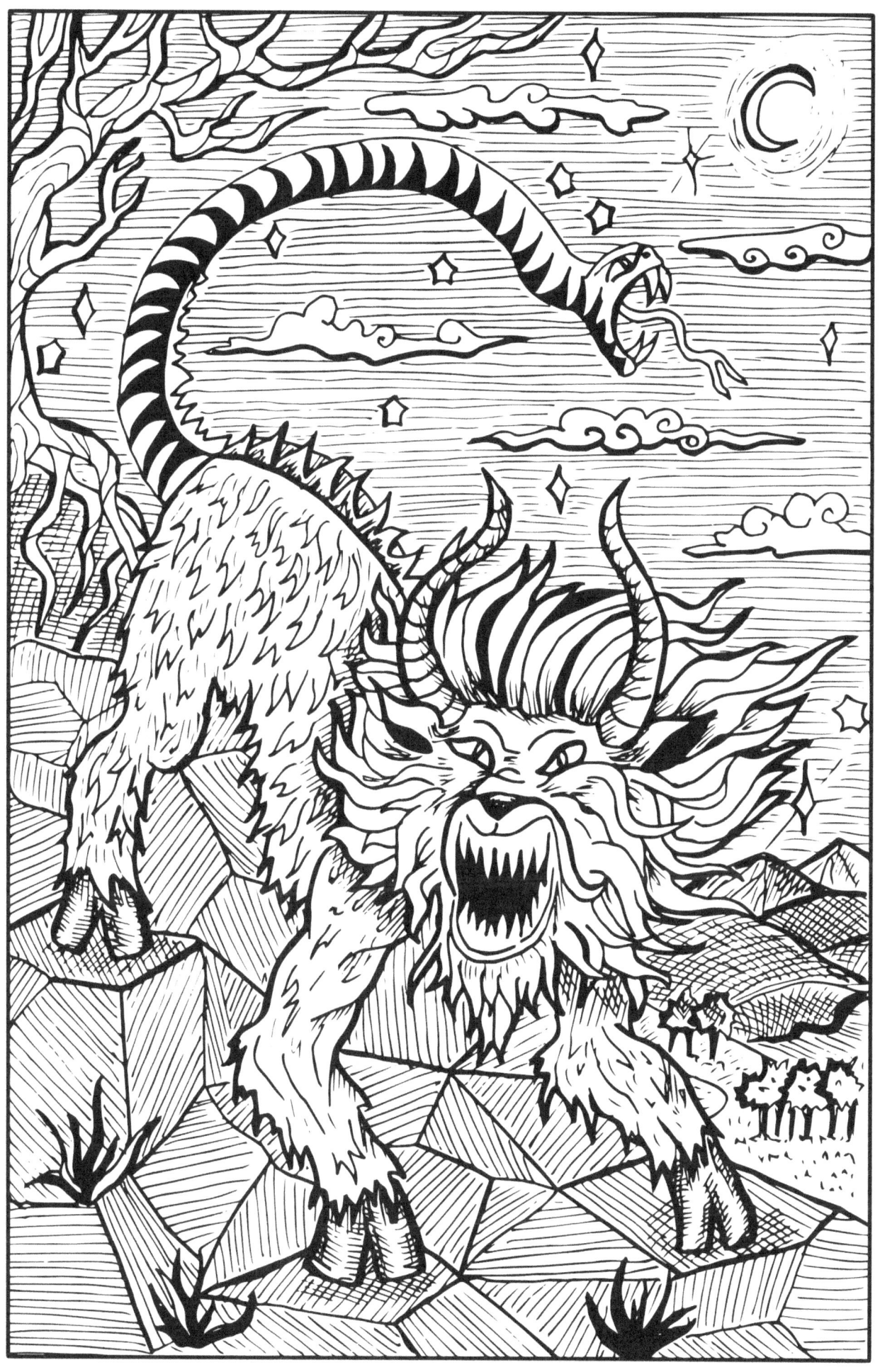

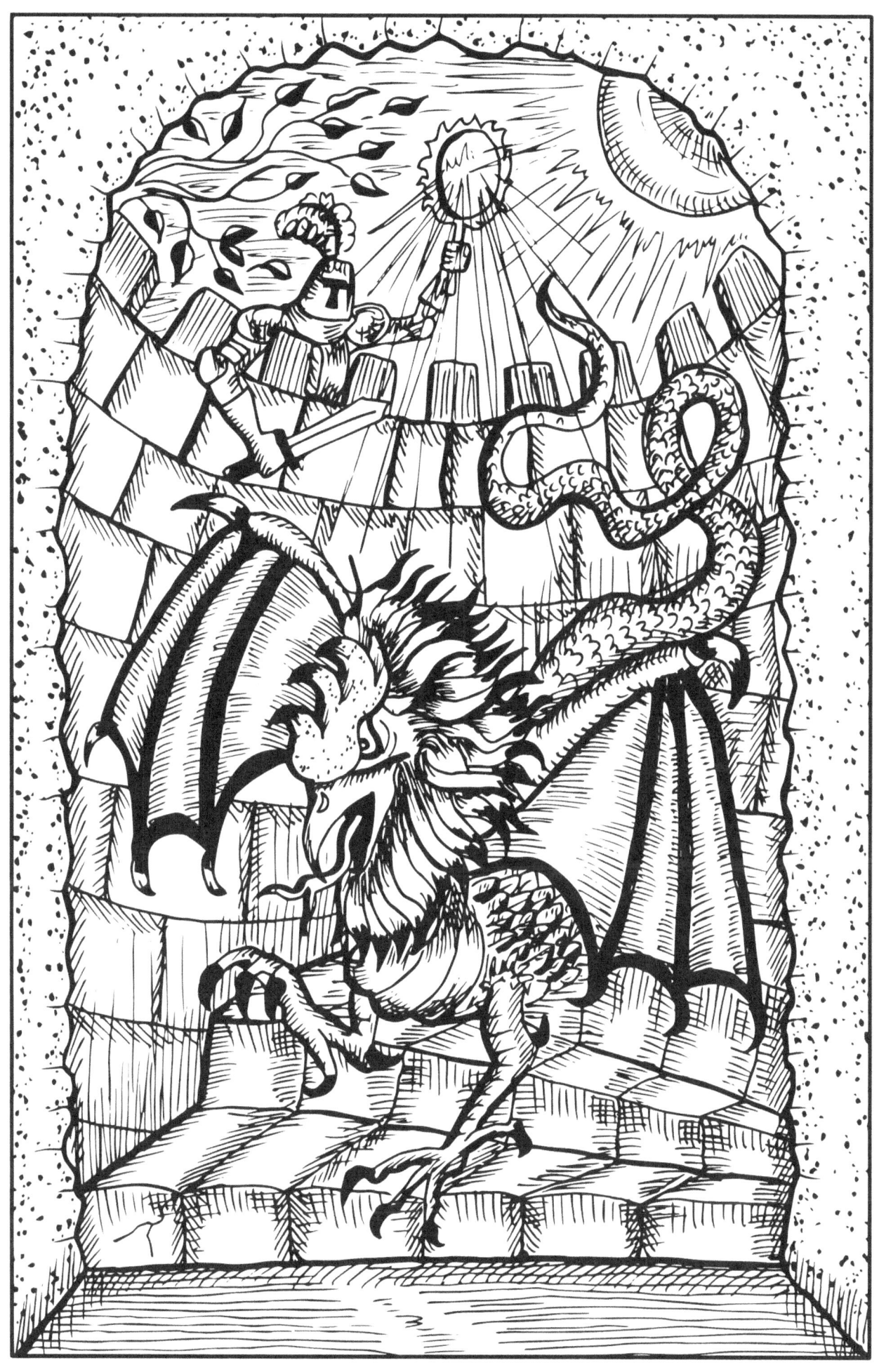

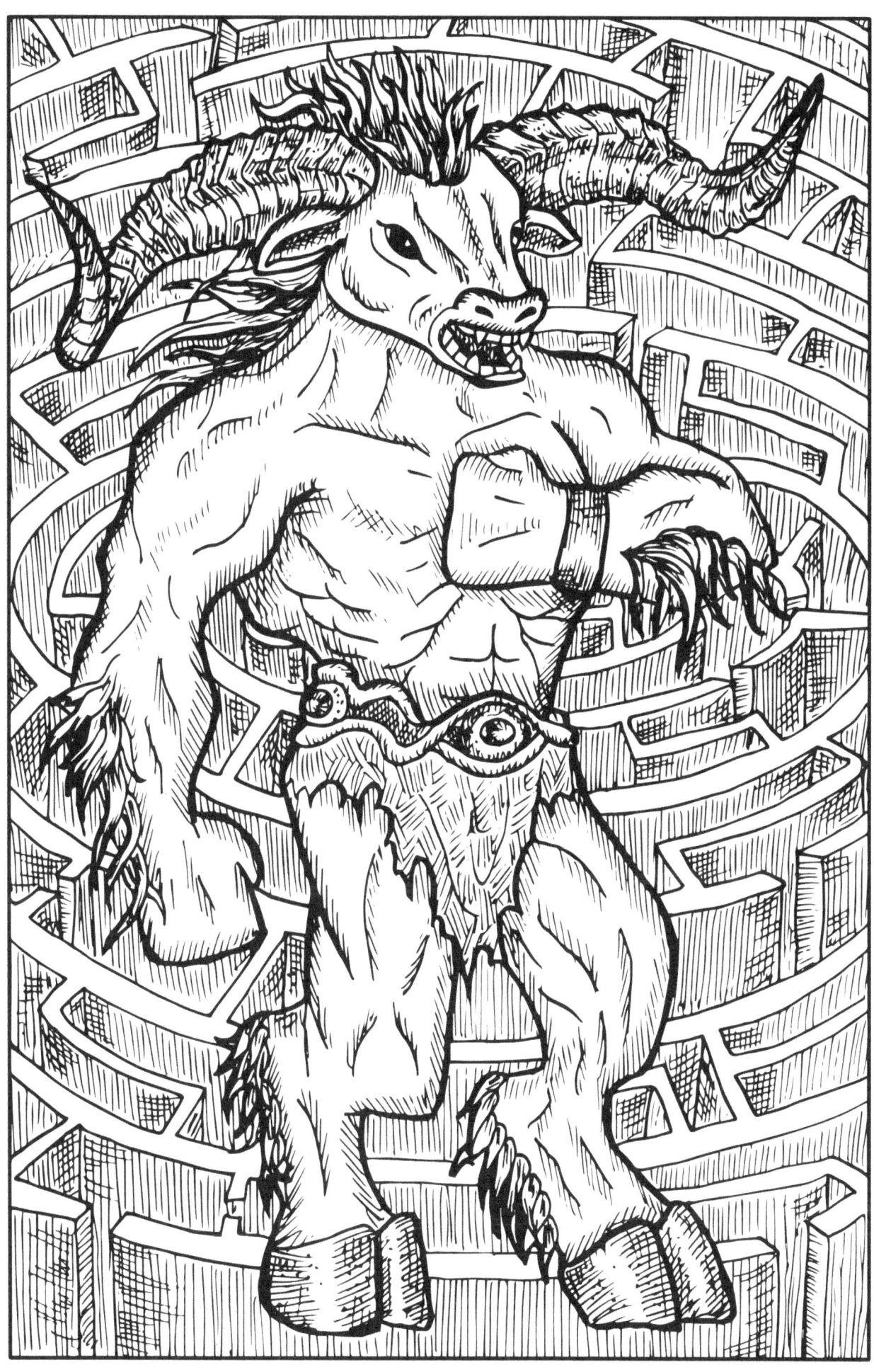

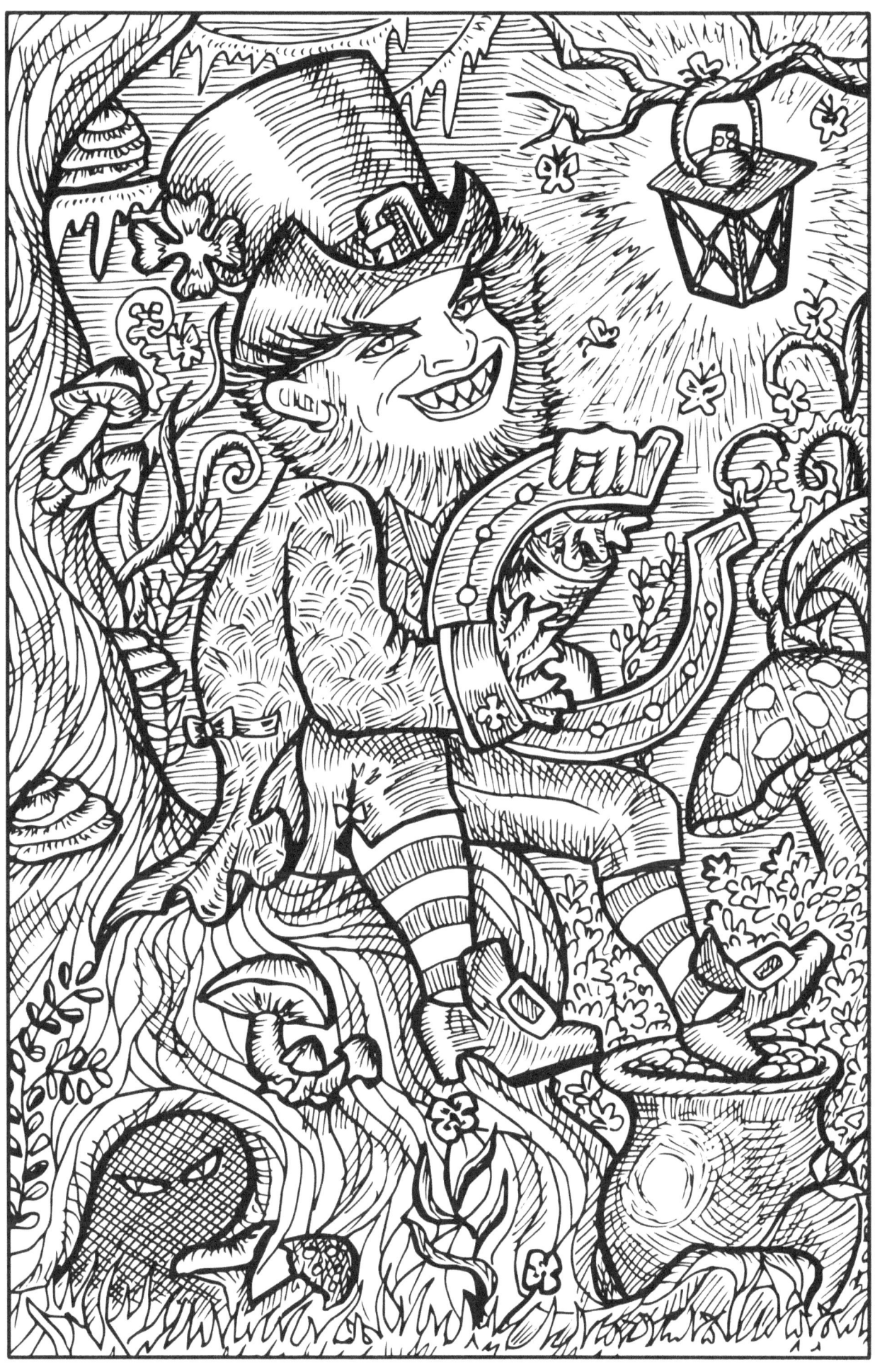

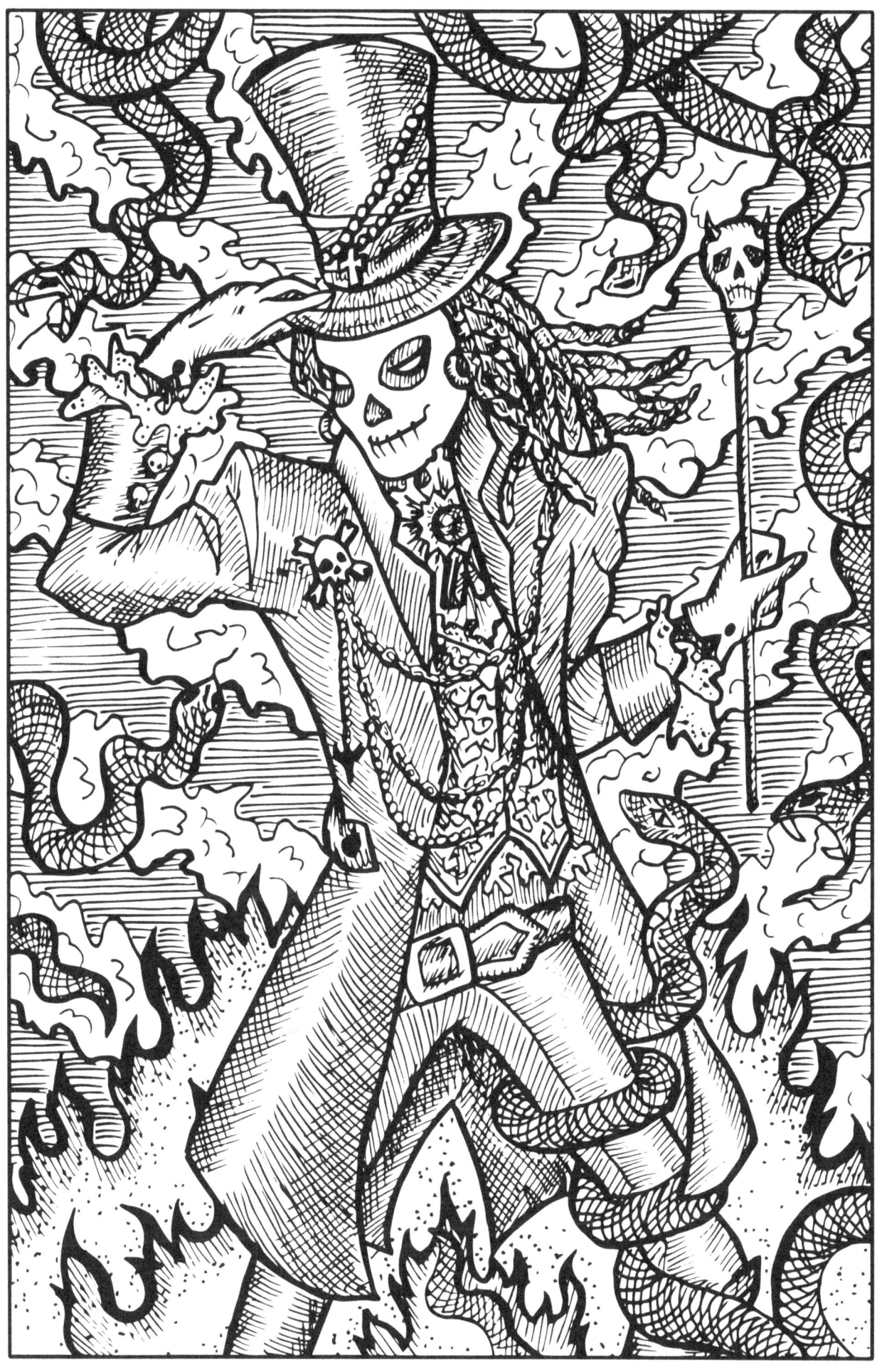

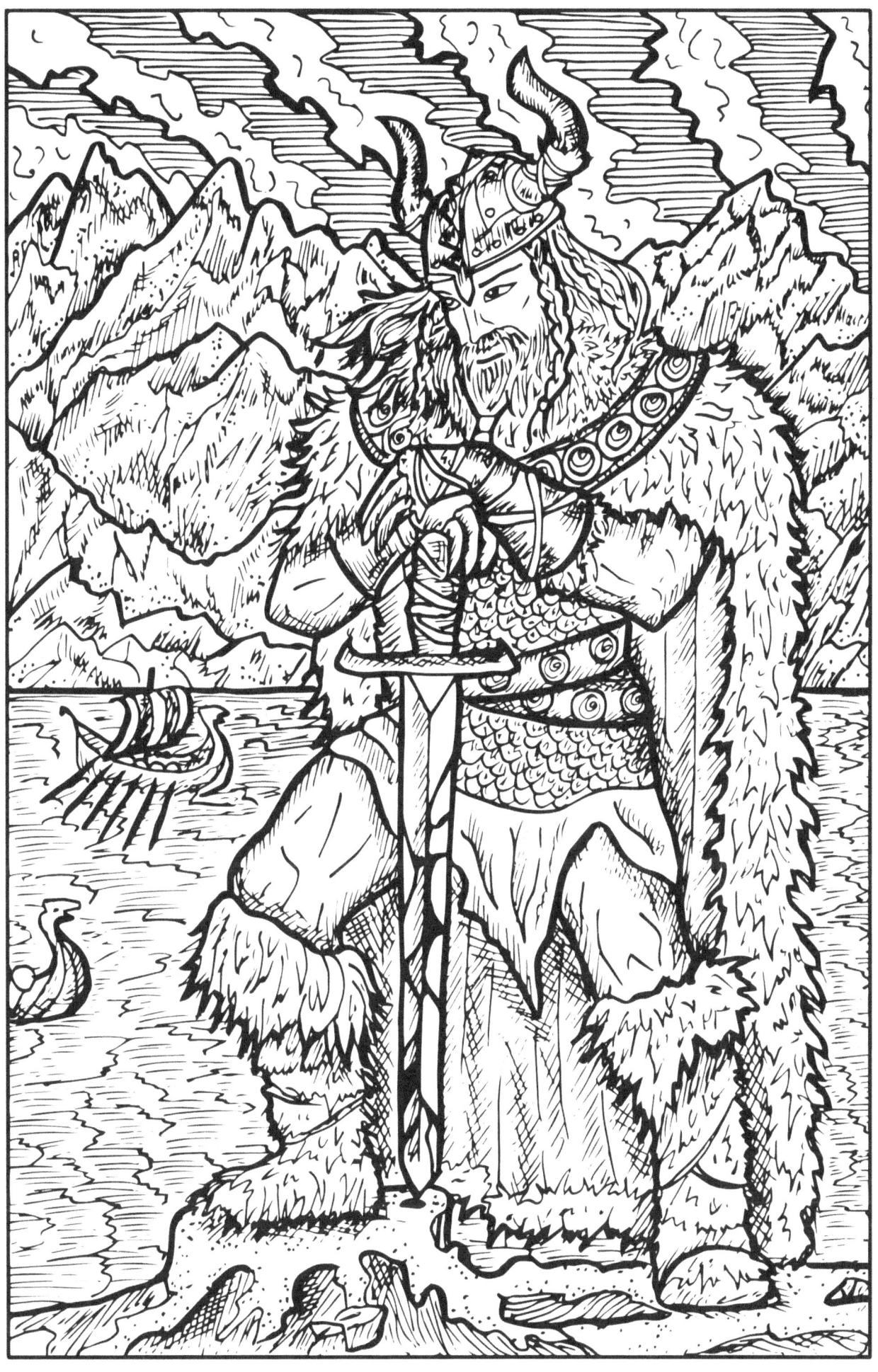

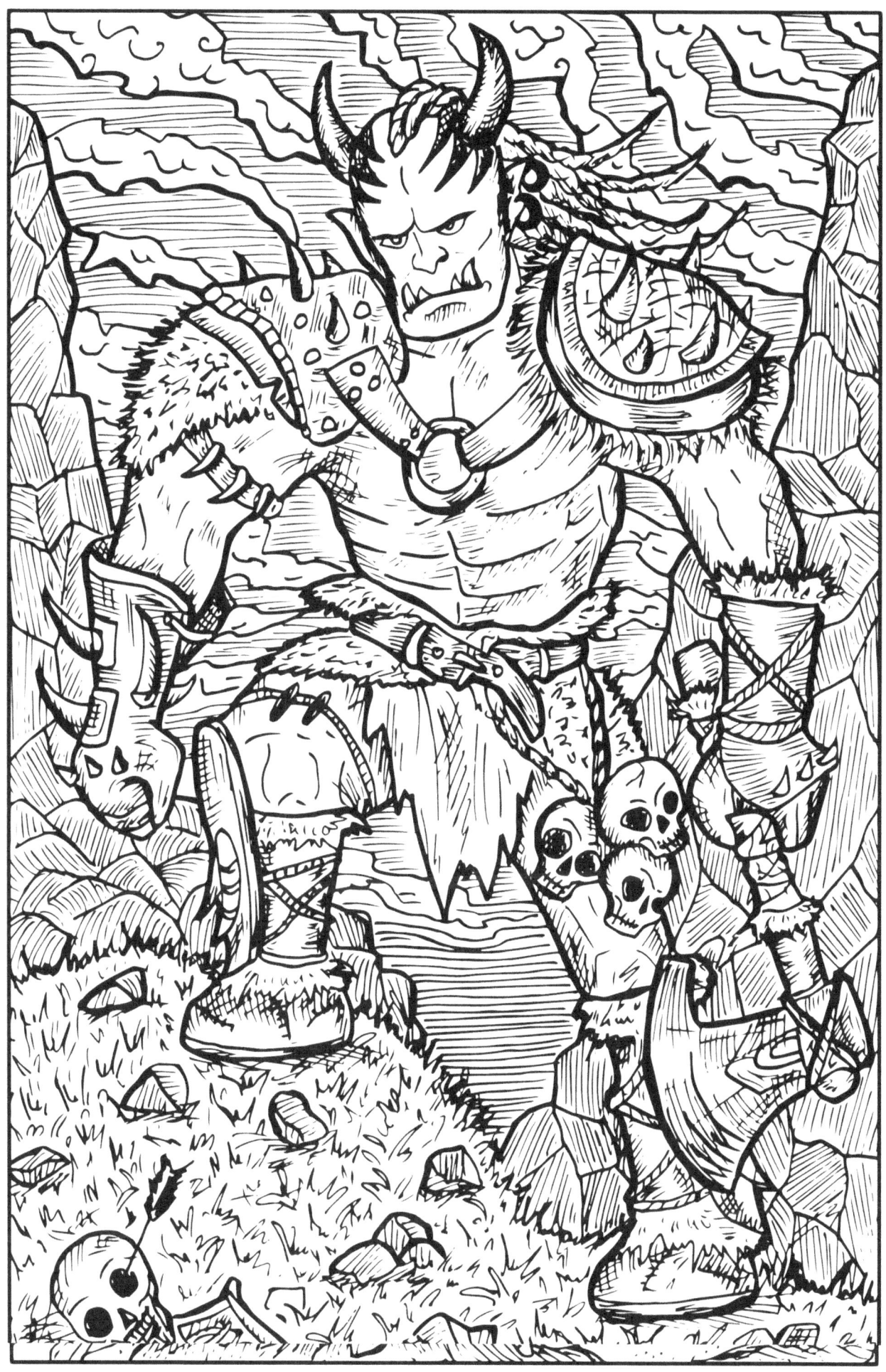

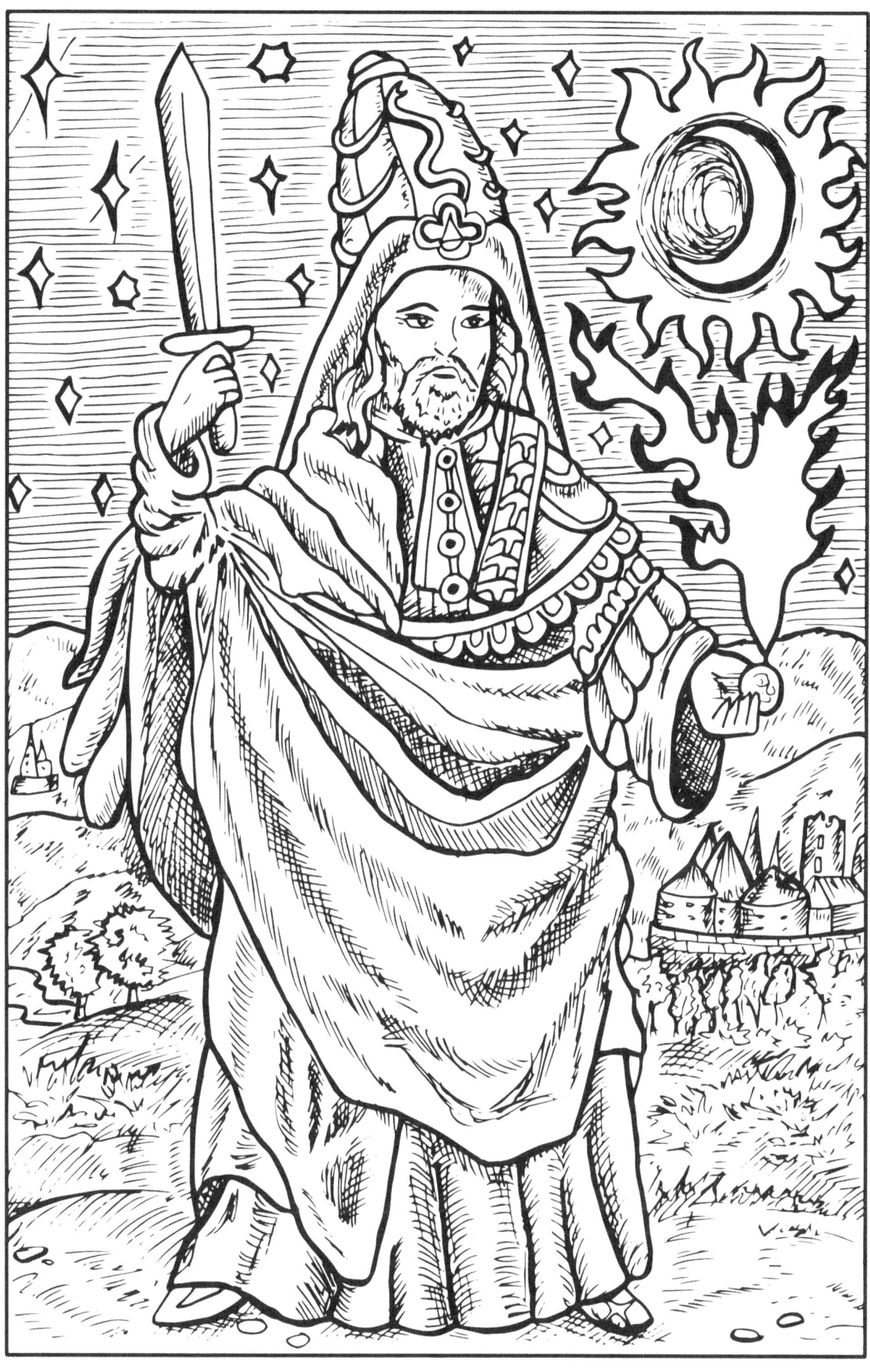

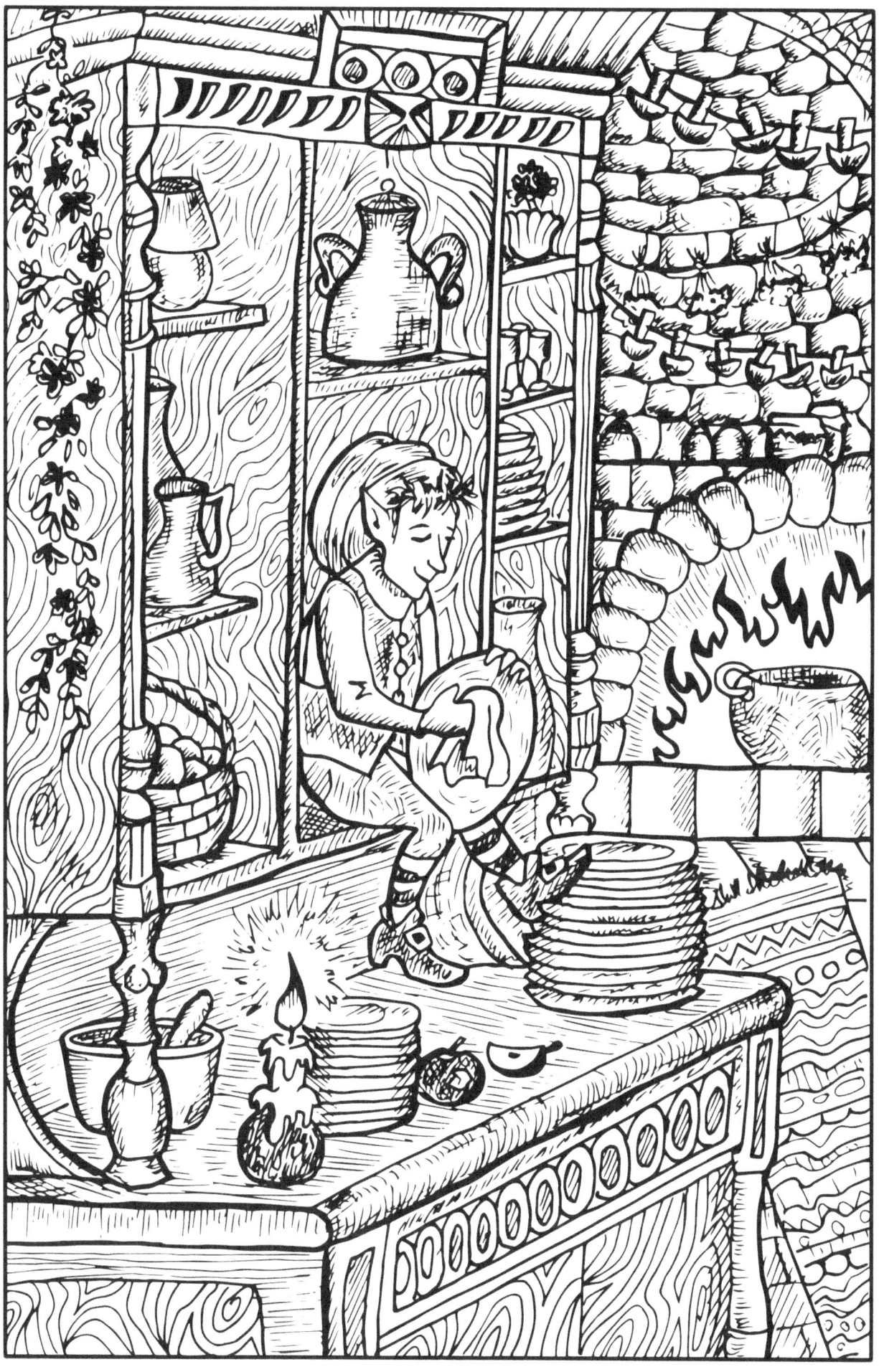

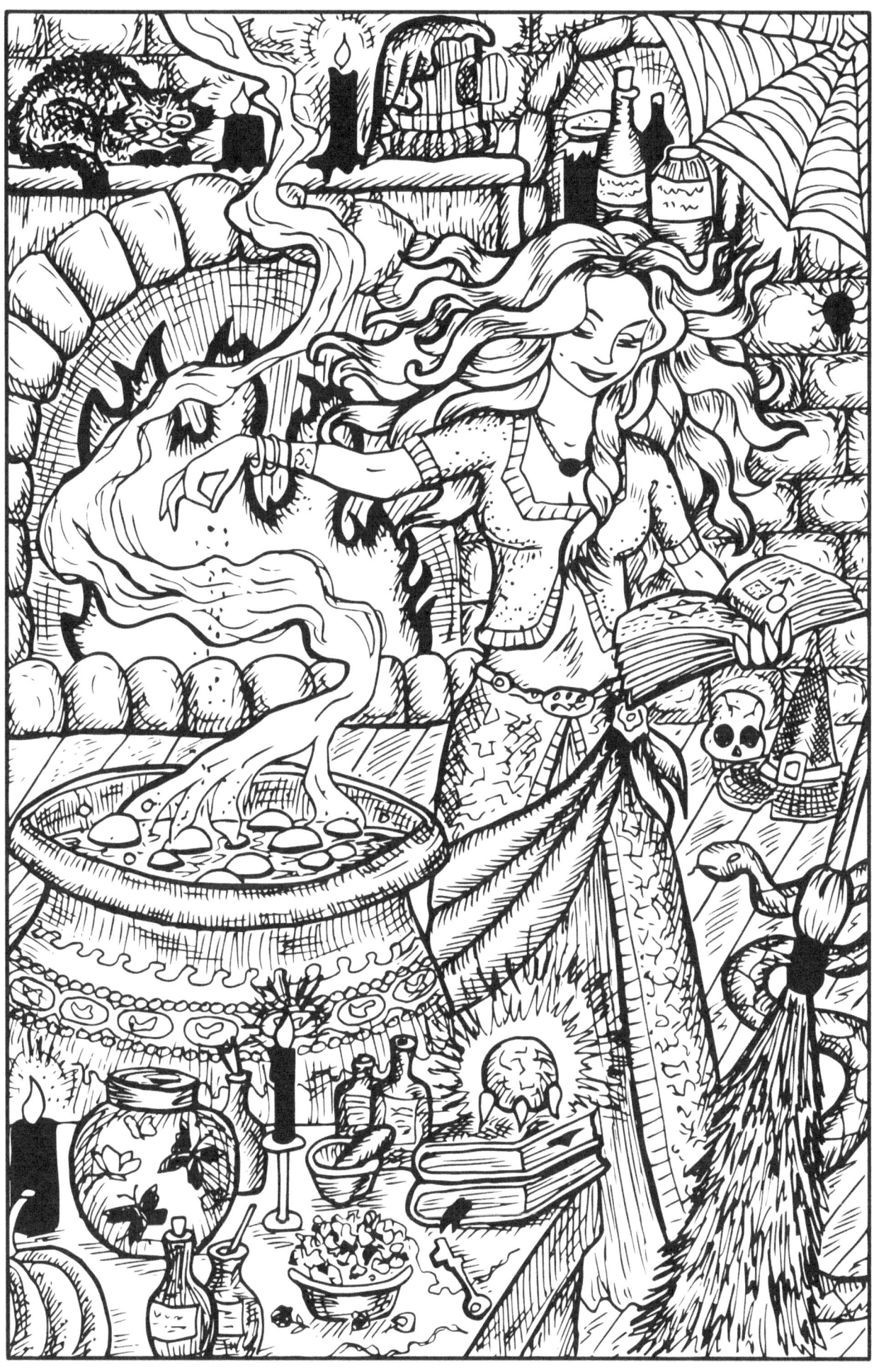

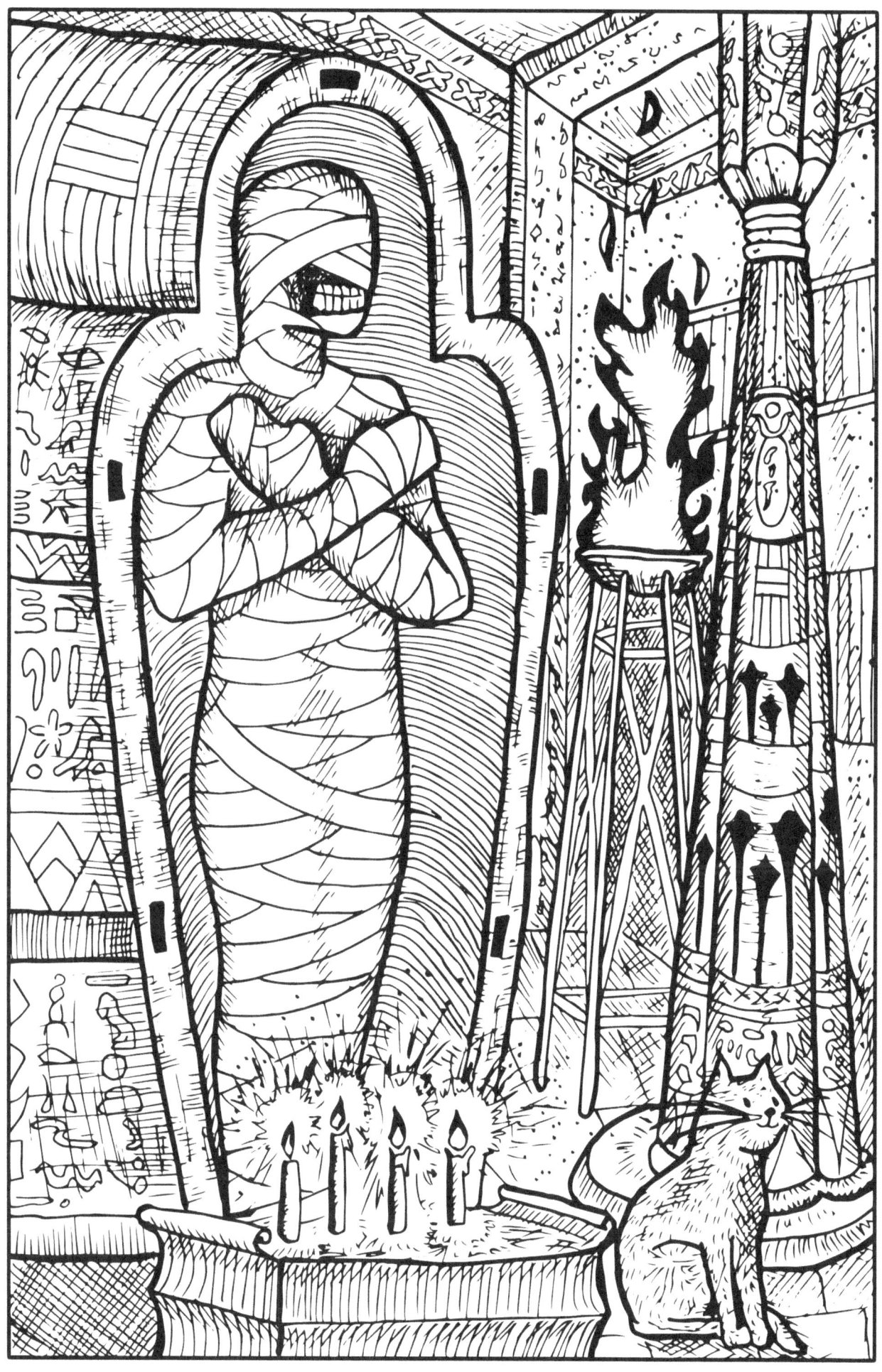

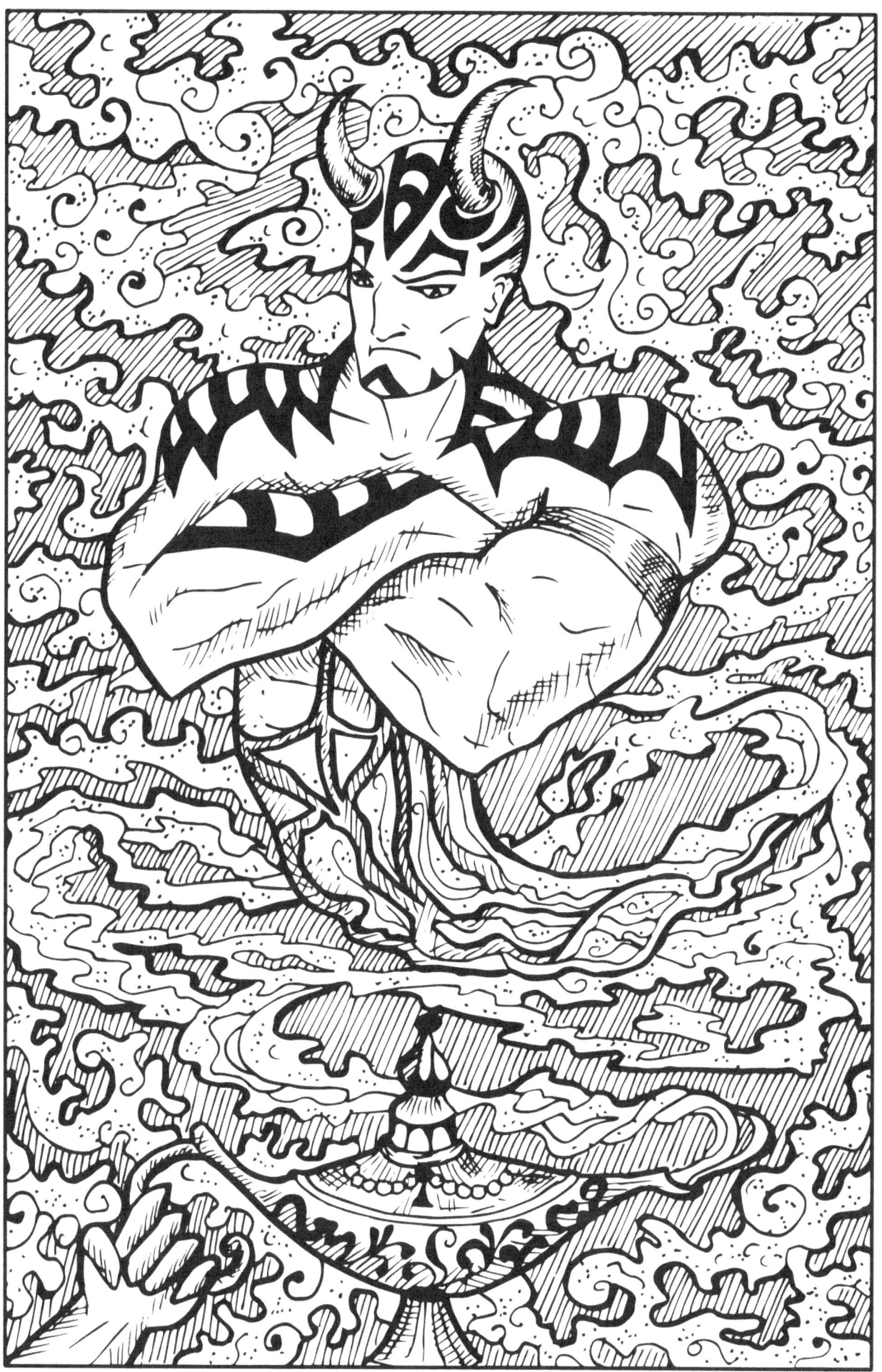

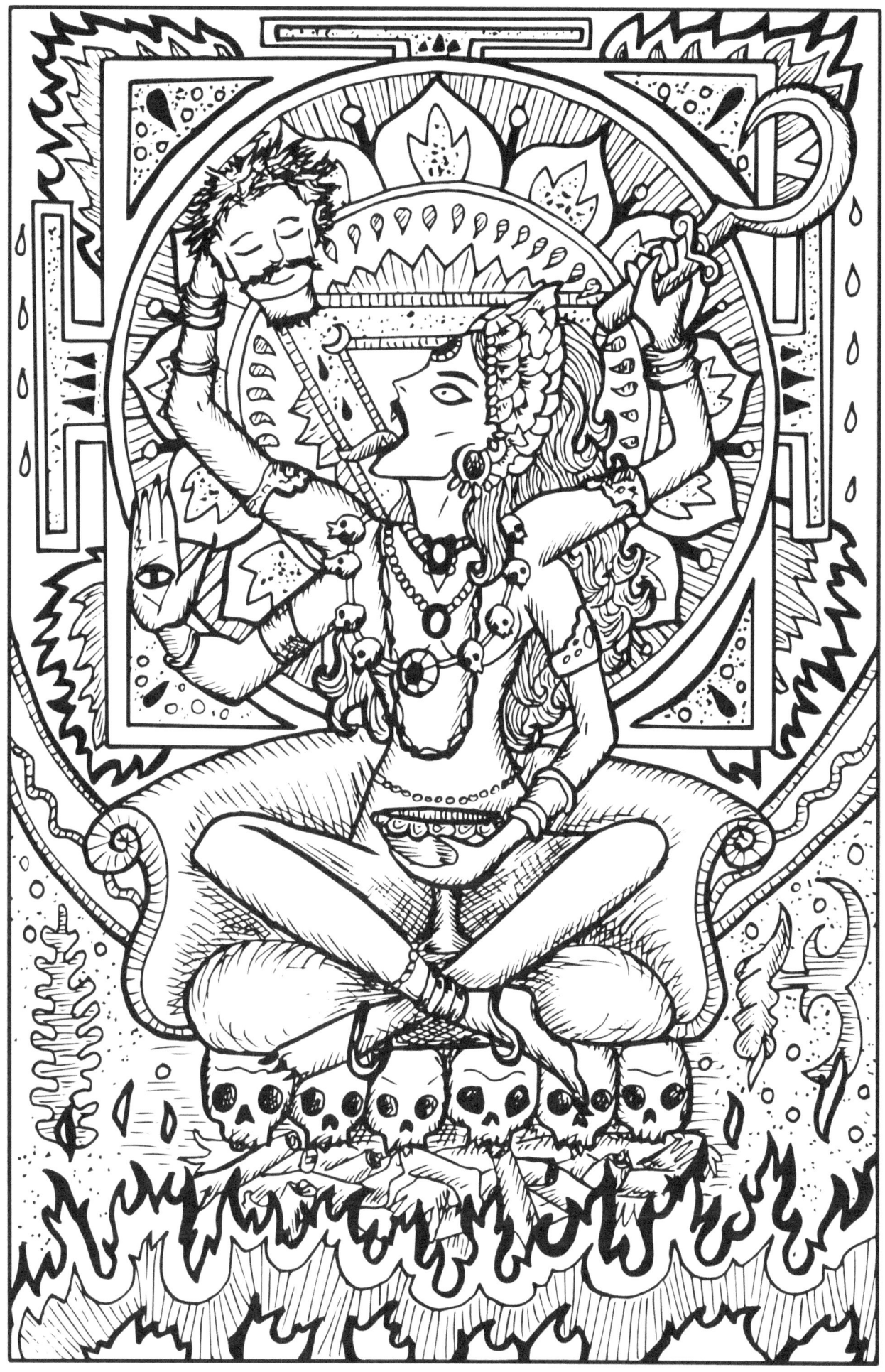

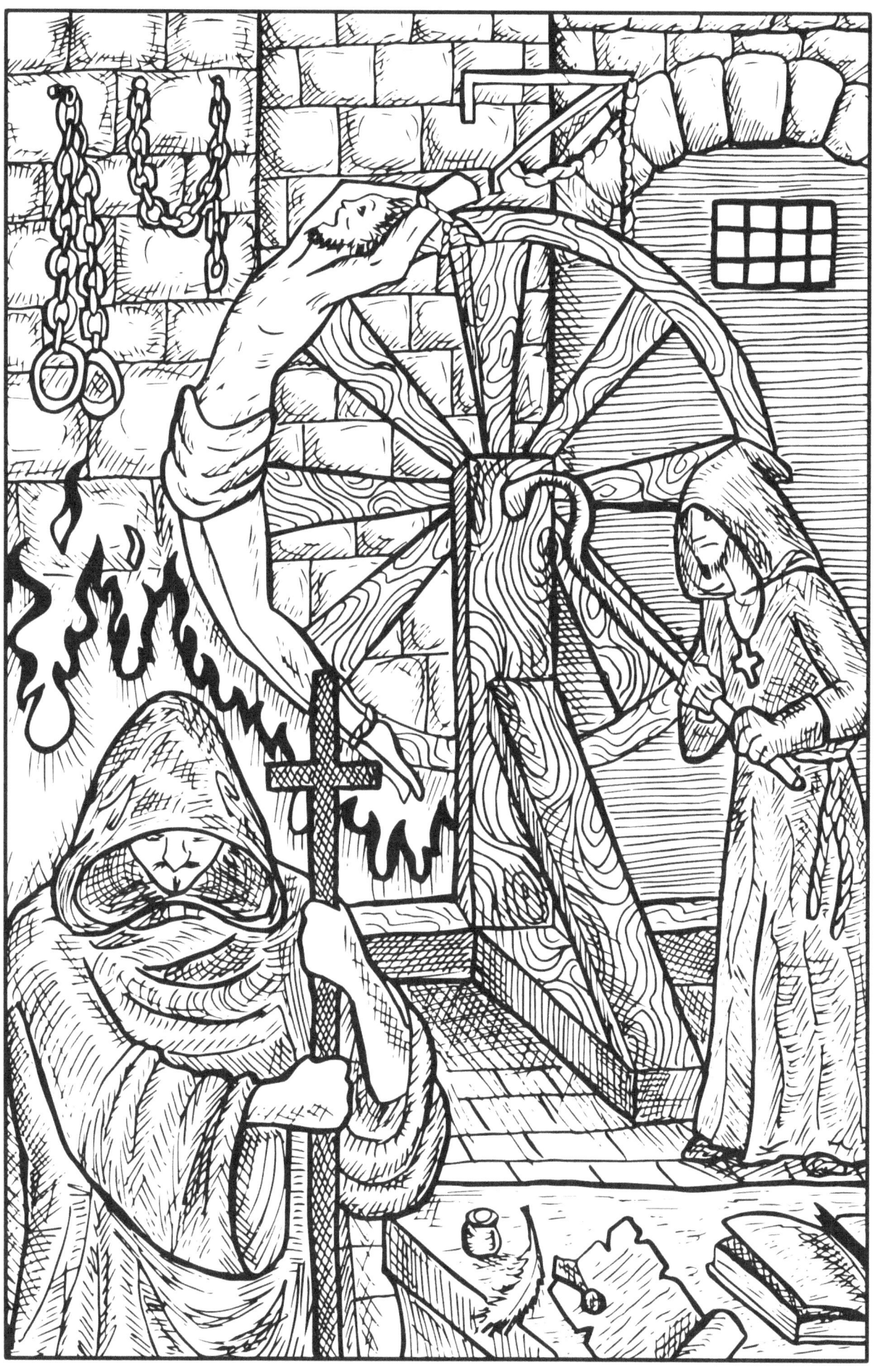

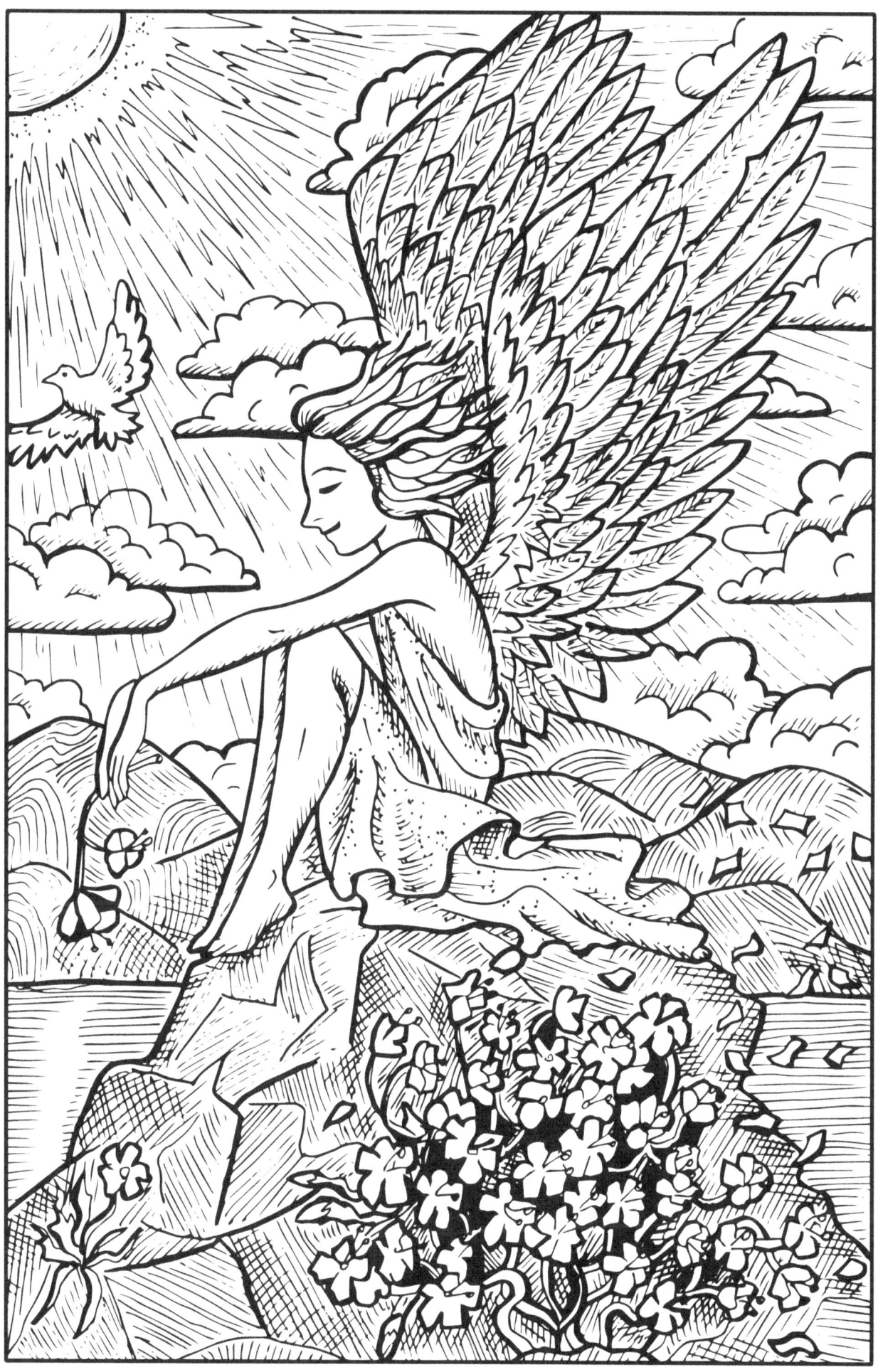

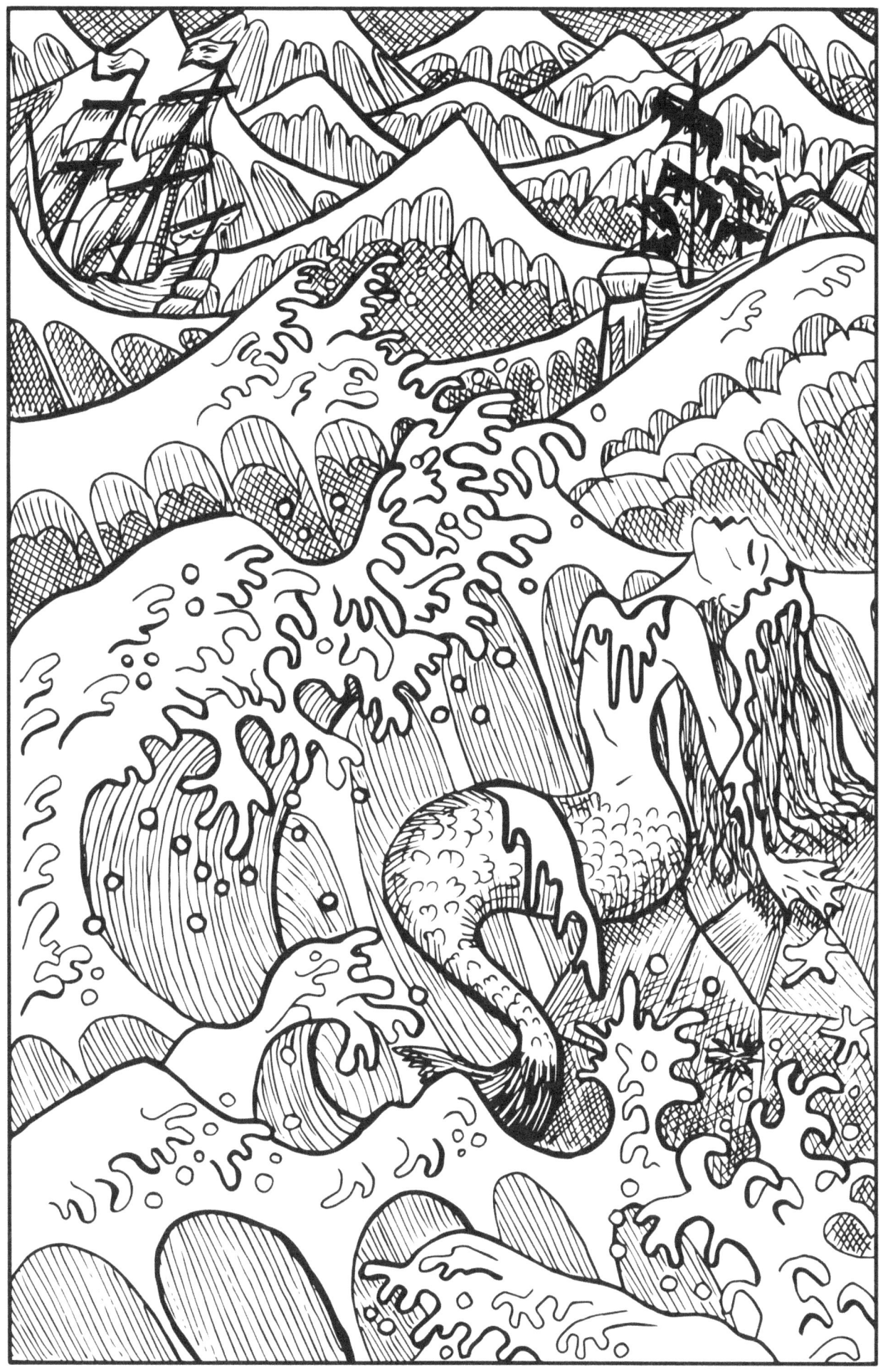

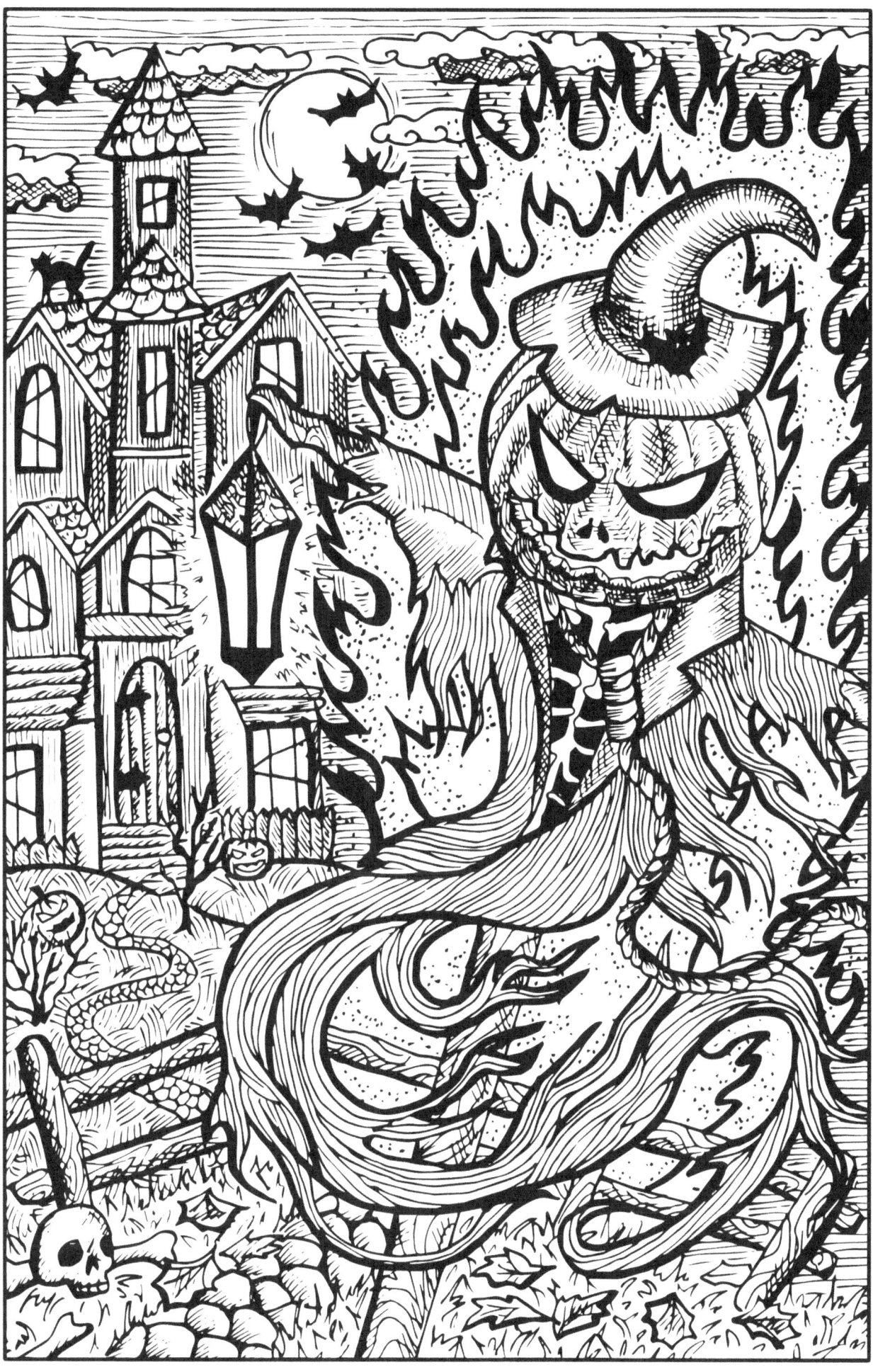

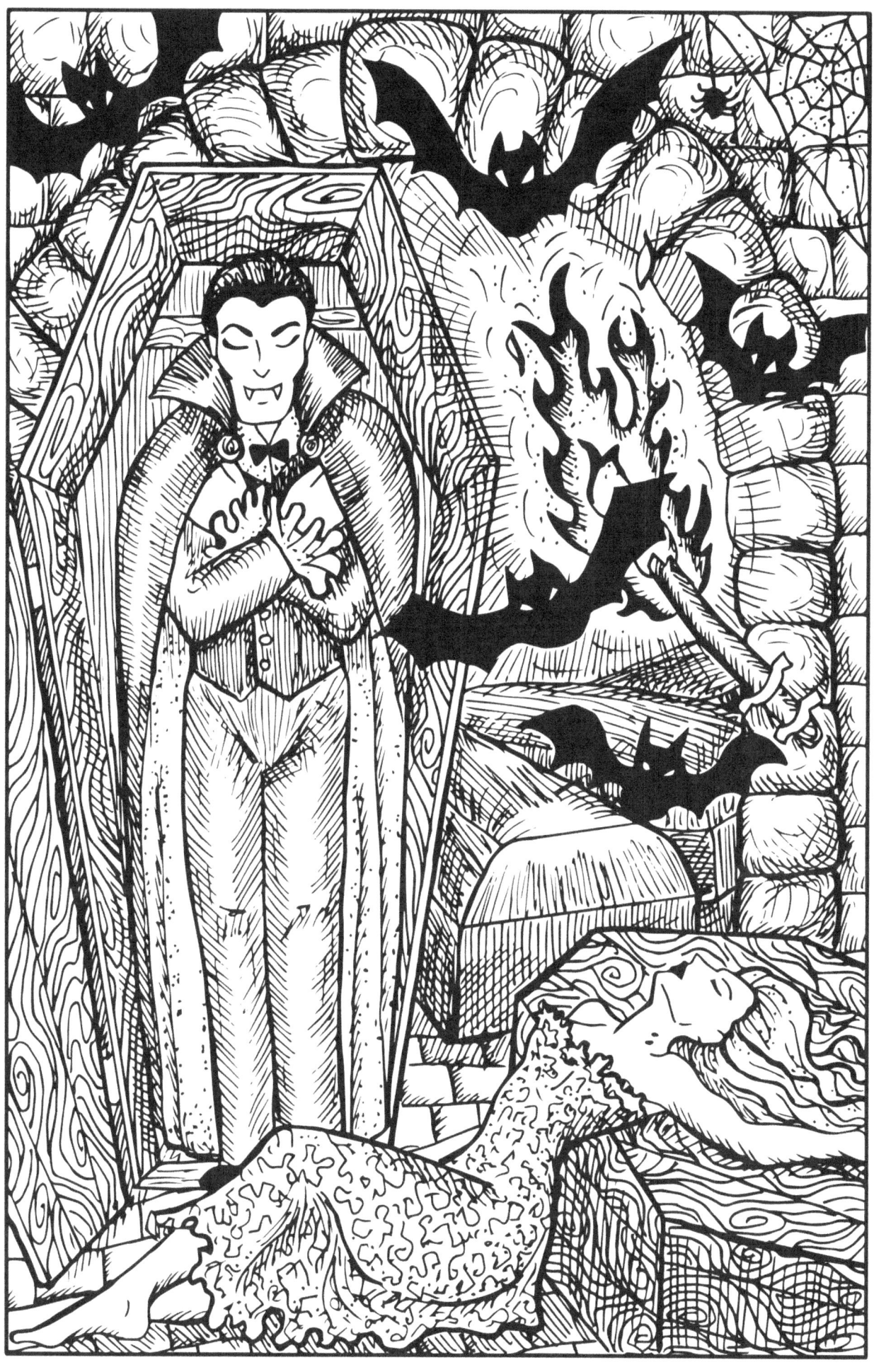

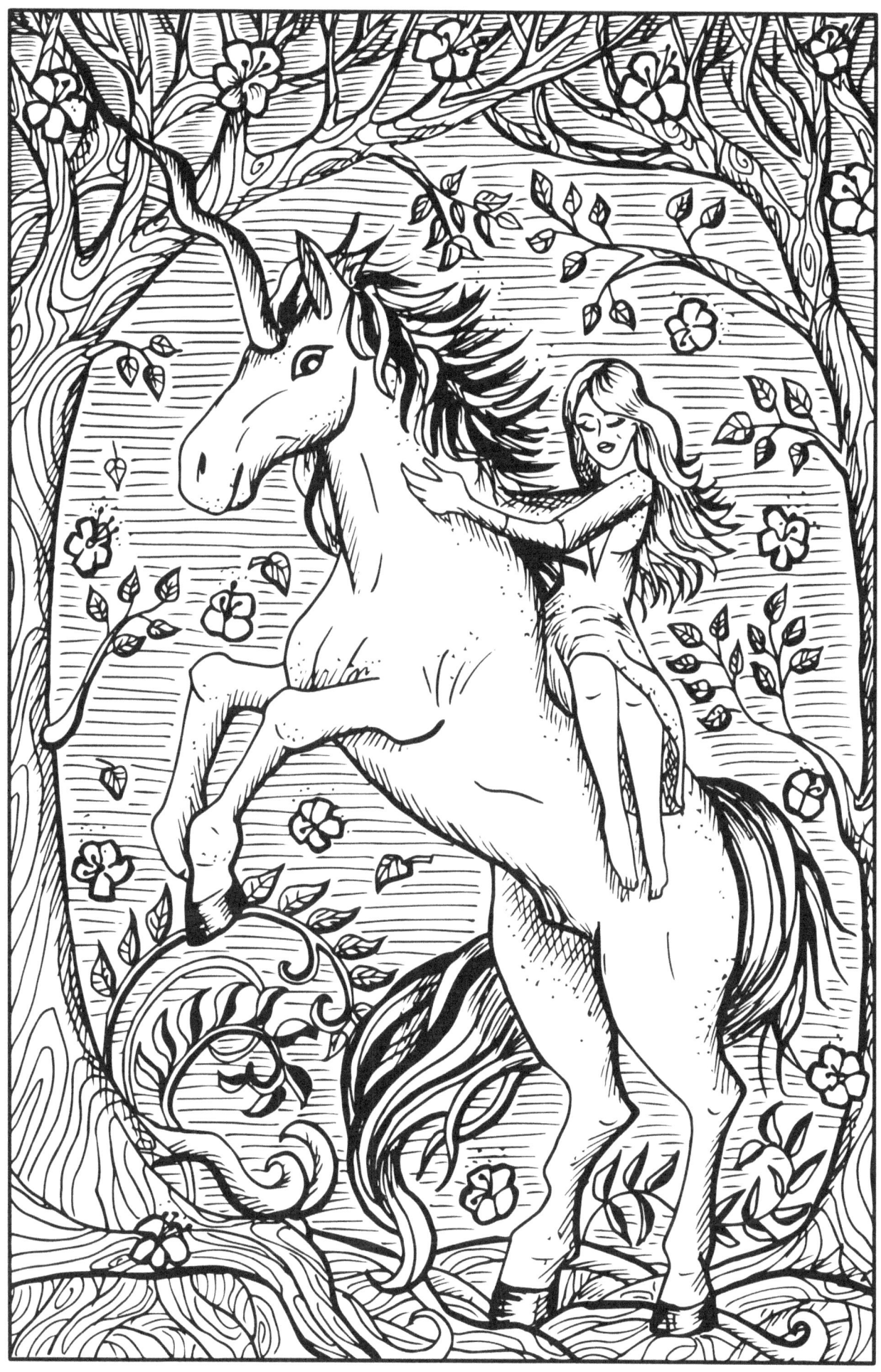

Fancy Coloring

NEW BOOKS AVAILABLE HERE

amazon.com/author/coloringcreator

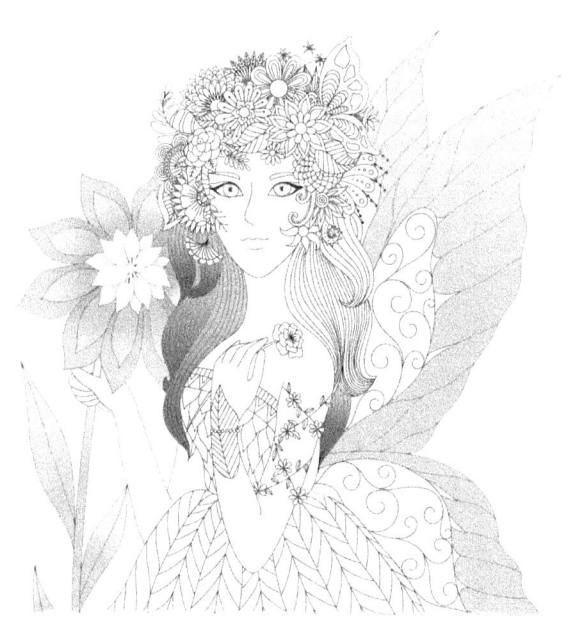

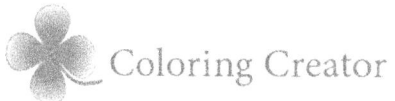
Coloring Creator

www.ingramcontent.com/pod-product-compliance
Lightning Source LLC
Chambersburg PA
CBHW080001230526
45470CB00008B/2821